I0122028

Laugh, Cry, Reflect

Stories from a Joyful Heart

Other books by Amy Laundrie:

Whinny of the Wild Horses
Eye of Truth
Thirty Pieces of Silver
Lead Us Not Into Temptation
Wolves in Sheep's Clothing
Noah's Ark Pet Care Club

Laugh, Cry, Reflect

Stories from a Joyful Heart

Amy Laundrie

HenschelHAUS Publishing, Inc.
Milwaukee, Wisconsin

Copyright © 2018 by Amy Laundrie
All rights reserved.

Published by
HenschelHAUS Publishing, Inc.
www.henschelHAUSbooks.com

ISBN: 978159598-607-8
E-ISBN: 9781595958-608-5
LCCN: 2018936032

Photo credits:
Cover art courtesy of © Can Stock Photo / tomwang
Photograph on p. 3 courtesy of Aaron Toth
Photograph on p. 6 courtesy of © Can Stock Photo / ehrlif
Photograph on p. 12 courtesy of Eric Grzenia
Photograph on p. 13 courtesy of © Can Stock Photo / 2002Lubava1981
Photograph on p. 21 courtesy of Ruth Ann Gundrum
Photograph on p. 46 courtesy of © Can Stock Photo / Anetlanda
Photographs on p. 25, 42, 58, 72, 73, 96, 111, 129, 142 courtesy of Amy Laundrie
Photograph on p. 60 courtesy of Sharon Minnick Burnaford
Photographs on p. 92, 119, 122, 134 courtesy of Frank Laundrie
Photograph on p. 93 courtesy of © Can Stock Photo / vmenshov
Artwork on p. 101 courtesy of Eleanor Palmer
Photograph on p. 105 courtesy of Marsha Dunlap's family
Artwork on p. 107 by Marsha Dunlap
Photograph on p. 126 courtesy of Dolphin Discovery Photo

Printed in the United States of America

*Dedicated to Gayle Rosengren and Gisela Hamm
for their continued faith, encouragement, and support.*

Table of Contents

Disclaimer

Please note, dear readers, and especially the police officer who pulled me over for speeding, this work is classified a memoir, but I admit to stretching the truth if it benefited the story. So officer, I didn't really plan on tricking you. Truly, I didn't.

Acknowledgments

Laugh, Cry, Reflect is a cause to celebrate and acknowledge all those who helped bring this book to life. Thanks to:

- my family, including my husband, Frank, children Jon, Heather, and Heidi, grandchildren and beyond

- my community in Wisconsin and *The Wisconsin Dells Events* and *The Vilas County News-Review* newspapers who published several of these columns

- my publisher Kira Henschel

- my proofreaders Gisela Hamm, Joan Bauer, Frank Laundrie, and Patti Notes

- and finally, my generous writing partners, especially those I've worked with for many years and who are my dear friends: Gayle Rosengren, Kathleen Ernst, Eileen Daily, Laurie Rosengren, Sharon Addy, Shelley Lueck, Lisl Detlefsen, Deborah Jacobs, Sue Berk Koch, Donna O'Keefe, Eva Apelqvist, Shawn McGuire, Liisa Eyerly, Susan Winstead, Shirley Tollacksen, Kat Abbott, Jen Reinfeld, and Amanda Coppedge Bosky.

Up Front and Personal

Two Peas on a Board

Two peas on a board. This phrase defined my teen years. The words were my high school boyfriend's. The peas were mine.

I've always been flatter than Nebraska, which gave me a completely different high school experience than that of the voluptuous girls. One warm summer day, my pimply faced boyfriend took me to a swim party. I threw on my two-year-old pink ruffled swimsuit. The ruffles were supposed to hide what I lacked, but let me tell you, they didn't.

The life of the party was a flirty, well-stacked girl whom I shall call BaBoom. This 36-D was a master at the game of seduction. She flitted around, giggling and bouncing when the boys tried to splash her. Testosterone was heavy in the air. When she leaned over to dip her hand in the pool, the boys salivated. BaBoom had the moves and power. She was a generously scooped hot fudge sundae. I was a plain vanilla cone wishing I could melt into the pool tiles.

Memories of BaBoom bounced around in my head when my husband and I celebrated our 25th anniversary in Hawaii. Waikiki Beach attracts the most gorgeous people on the planet. Every other man was a possible Mr. Universe. Every other woman had an hourglass figure and big, bouncy babooms. Was there something in the water? I began drinking glassfuls.

Soon after we returned home, I went in for my annual gynecology exam. My doctor found a lump and suspicious lymph nodes. I agonized for a week, feeling the lump, sure it was growing. The doctor wanted me to see a specialist, who advised a mammogram. The day of the exam the lump felt enormous. Agonizing hours that became days followed. Meanwhile, an acquaintance began chemotherapy for breast cancer. A coworker with a son still in elementary school died from breast cancer. I couldn't help wondering if I would suffer the same fate.

The day the clinic finally called to say the lump was only a harmless cyst, I celebrated. I threw back my shoulders showing off my small, healthy breasts.

A Simpler Time in My Plymouth Valiant

I loved my Plymouth Valiant

*W*hile waiting for the light to change, I pulled up alongside a man driving an antique blue Plymouth Valiant. My first car had been a turquoise Valiant. I wondered if this one, too, had the cool push buttons for neutral, reverse, and drives 1, 2, and 3.

The light changed, and I paused in my uninspiring Ford to let the Valiant pull ahead. As I followed it, years faded away. When I drove my old Valiant through the neighborhood with the windows down, (it didn't have air conditioning or a radio) the world was a quieter place. Many women were stay-at-home moms. Dogs didn't bark to get out of pens because they freely roamed around their yards. No car alarms blared, no telemarketers called, and no text messages buzzed. I was free to drive in silence, to think, imagine, and plan.

My big worries then were how to wrap angora around my boyfriend's class ring, who would be at Friday night's football game, and which station had gas for less than $.25 a gallon. My hair was swept up in a ponytail instead of moussed, blow-dried, and highlighted. I drove my girlfriends to the ice cream stand and ordered a chocolate shake, not worrying about carbs or calories. When I said, "My aching back," I didn't mean it literally and necking had nothing to do with keyboard strain.

Ah, yes. Then, a person could just turn the TV dial rather than sort through the multiple remotes trying to figure out whether to power-up the DVD, DVR or choose streaming. My favorite show was Marlo Thomas' *That Girl*. I attended slumber parties where we watched TV for hours, drinking cherry Kool-Aid, giggling, and picking at our split ends. When the clock struck midnight, the TV station played *The Star Spangled Banner* and the screen grew fuzzy. The world was better at shutting down in those days.

When I drove my Valiant no one had a Smartphone or a PC. A mouse was something that made a nest under the hood unless my dad sprinkled mothballs there, and viruses didn't send people to the technology department, but to bed.

The Valiant's turn signal blinked. *No!* I wanted to shout. *Don't go! I want to keep following you.* When I was driving my Valiant, the only terrorist in my life was my adolescent brother. The number of bombings was relatively low unless my dog had brought fleas onto the living room carpet and we needed to fumigate again. What shocked the world was the gyrations of Elvis's hips and the length of the Beatles' hair. Ah, let me put on my pedal-pushers and once again get behind that wheel.

The Peignoir Set

Peignoir set

I've kept the filmy, red negligee and matching robe for over twenty years. Given to me by my husband's sister as an engagement gift, I've displayed the expensive ensemble on a wooden rack that hangs on the bedroom wall. I've never worn it. It's too big in the wrong places, too sheer, and just not me. Yet it held such promise.

With the approach of another birthday, realism hit, and I decided the time had come to give it up. I opened the donation bag wide, picked up the crimson silk and tried to drop it in. The fabric floated away. Just before it reached the bag, I quickly snatched it back. I spread it out in my lap.

Why do I feel this way? Is it because this ensemble is everything I'll never be: vivacious and exotic, young and impulsive, suggestive and flirtatious, a combination of Madonna and Angelina Jolie? I sigh. The woman wearing this peignoir set should be hosting Saturday night dinner parties, regularly buying fresh flowers, scheduling manicures and massages, and doing something about these aging wrinkles. She should be meeting friends for drinks at chandelier-lit bars and talking about her latest cruise to an exotic island or her week at a romantic ski resort. Her closet should be filled with high heels in various colors and styles instead of sensible oxfords with orthopedic inserts.

I stand swishing the fabric so it seems to dance. The woman wearing this gown should be the center of attention as she waltzes or tangos across the dance floor. She should have a handsome man inviting her to share a bottle of fine Cabernet Sauvignon at his Italian villa or whisking her away to New York for the premier of the latest Broadway show. She shouldn't have achy legs, arthritic toes, or a widening waistline. She shouldn't have fallen arches, age spots, or this feeling of loss.

I stroke the gown and robe again, but this time when I drop them into the bag, I force myself to let them stay. I swallow, a soft ache in my throat. I'll never be asked to be a guest on the *Oprah Show* for my fine contributions to humanity. I'll never work a crowd charming people with my witticisms. I'll never be a jet-setter or comfortably enjoy extravagance. Even if I would gain weight in the right places, this peignoir set would never fit me.

I drive to the resale store. When the helper is finally able to pry the bag from my arms, I slowly turn away.

Tomorrow, I'll count my blessings for my rich, happy life and all that I am. I'll remember I still have dreams to fulfill. I'll look forward to the future that includes travel, fulfilling work, and the love of my long-time husband. I'll realize unexpected adventures await and joys beyond imagining, including watching my children and grandchildren grow and discover who they are.

But for now I take one last look back at the donation bag and pause a moment to mourn for all I'll never be.

Swiftly Flow the Days

I thought I was prepared for the day of my younger daughter's wedding. I'd bought a new dress and shoes, sampled the lemon chicken and wedding cake, and planned the flower centerpieces for the reception table. Now if only I could keep my emotions in check.

While watching the beautician style Heidi's hair, the years melted away. The refrain from *The Fiddler on the Roof* resounded in my head, Tevia's words rising to my throat. "Sunrise, Sunset. Swiftly flow the days." I sniffled, but managed to keep my mascara from running.

The beautician fussed with a curl and I clearly recalled taking Heidi for her first big-girl haircut right before nursery school. I'd collected a piece of her white-blonde hair and taped it in her baby book. I chuckle to myself as another memory comes to mind. When she was a bit older, I'd allowed a friend in beautician school to perm Heidi's hair. We attended an outdoor party shortly after and when the host's sheepdog saw her curls, so much like a sheep's, he watched her every move. As Heidi tried to leave the group of partiers, the dog darted off, lunging at her, herding her back to the others.

When Heidi's hair was finished, we headed to the church where her bridesmaids helped her into her elegant dress. The words to *Sunrise, Sunset*, jumbled in emotion, rearranged themselves in my mind.

"Is this the little peanut I carried? When did "the Hyder" get to be such a beauty? Wasn't it yesterday when she was sleeping in my arms?"

Was this vision in taffeta the same girl who rode horseback and raised baby bunnies, who loved wearing scary Halloween masks and was head monster at the tourist attraction Dungeon of Horrors?

Heidi was great at scaring people whether intentionally or unintentionally. The worst shock for me was when, as a preteen, she asked if we could go to the store and buy a home pregnancy kit. It was a long time before I could find my voice. "Uh, why do you want a home pregnancy kit?"

"To see if my rabbit is pregnant."

I let out a long, grateful breath.

For the wedding, Heidi wore her beloved grandmother's pearls. At the age of five, she once cued in on her grandmother's hearing loss and, eyes sparkling with fun, told me the reason she hadn't done the requested chore was that her hearing aids weren't working.

Heidi has always been good with one-liners. Because of problems with her knees, the doctor advised her to quit the basketball team. She told us, "I'm not good in spelling and you won't let me quit that."

She remained in basketball and during the last game when the team, wanting to thank her for her loyalty, tossed her the ball so she could make the final basket, I didn't think I could feel any more proud. I was wrong.

The usher seated me. We rose and faced the back of the church. My husband Frank walked Heidi down the aisle. Most people, I'm sure, saw a beautiful, elegant woman in taffeta and pearls, but I saw a hundred moments in time.

She and her soon-to-be husband looked deep into one another's eyes as they said their vows. After they kissed, they walked together down the aisle and greeted everyone. I gave a long sigh, relieved I hadn't cried.

Frank and I watched as the photographer positioned our children. Jon, a loving father and husband, hardworking and responsible, stood on Heidi's left. Heather, sophisticated and accomplished, with convictions that will make this world a better place, stood to Heidi's right. As the photographer set up, they lovingly teased one another. A lump formed in my throat and I silently echoed the song's phrase: *Swiftly flow the days*. Through misty eyes, I saw our children, all grown up, wrap arms around one another and pose for the camera. Unprepared for the rush of emotions, I let the tears flow.

My children, Heather, Heidi, and Jon

My Purse: Mirror to the Soul Or
Where the Heck Are My Car Keys?

*I*f the purse is the mirror to a woman's soul, I'm afraid mine needs polishing. I dump the contents out on a tray and begin sorting.

- aspirin
- dental floss
- nail files
- allergy pills (I don't have allergies but relatives do)
- anti-diarrhea tablets (Don't laugh; you may be running to me for these someday)

Ah, here's my grandson's missing dinosaur.

Hmpphh! So that's where I put that milk card. If I'd gotten it punched yesterday, I could have gotten a free gallon.

As I look at the pile, I marvel at how some women manage to carry those cute, tiny purses. Aren't they afraid they'll be caught without two Chapsticks, or their choice of three lipsticks? I neatly put the lipsticks back inside, including the freebie I got, which is an awful orange color but heck, it's brand new and I certainly can't throw it away.

It's not that I want to suffer from droopy purse shoulder. But how can I leave the house without supplies such as this shopping pouch? Stuffed inside are directions to the dog park (it's hard to find and I intend to go there someday) and coupons, only a few of which are expired. This pouch also includes a magazine picture of a swimsuit style that supposedly will hide my figure flaws—yeah, right.

I continue taking inventory.

- Band-Aids
- address labels
- paper in case I get a writing idea
- gum
- chocolate

- prescription sunglasses
- extra pair of glasses (hey, one pair could break)
- phone
- car and house keys
- lotion
- comb
- a pocket calendar
- moist wipes
- artificial sugar packets
- coffee packet in case I need a fix
- 7 earplugs

Although it doesn't seem logical to carry seven ear plugs, they do come in handy for noisy motel rooms or places where the music is cranked up to ear-aching decibels, and what if I lost one or two or, um, five?

The last item on the tray is my messy wallet. I take a peek inside at the rumpled cards, some of which are for defunct businesses and decide I'll save cleaning the wallet out for another day.

I scan the discard pile.

- old cough drop
- linty mint
- three expired coupons

I lift my purse. Much lighter.

My husband comes in and I show him my organized purse. "Yeah, that's great. So I need your keys to move your car."

I set it down and look inside. I dig and dig and dig. He shakes his head.

"I know they're in here somewhere," I mumble. Finally, I dump everything out. "Ah, yes, right here next to my contact case."

"Contact case? You haven't worn contacts for years."

I shrug. "Yeah, but if I start again, I'll know where to find them."

Caught Speeding? Plan Your Creative Excuse

I was speeding home on a dark, deserted road when stationary headlights caught my eye. Squad car? I glanced down and braked. 37 mph in a 25. The headlights pulled out.

You may know that sinking feeling. As the lights tailed me, I thought of possible excuses. Maybe I could use the one an officer from Adams County shared with me. The speeder had been camping and her car was full of mosquitoes. "When I slap my ankles," she explained, "my foot accidentally pushes down on the accelerator." I searched for bugs. Drat, not a one. The police lights were still there, though. My mind scrambled for other excuses.

That same Adams County officer had once told a speeder that he'd used aircraft radar to clock him. The man had said, "Aircraft! I suppose you S.O.B.s have submarines, too." The officer was tempted to warn the speeder to watch it when he crossed the Wisconsin River so he wouldn't get pulled over by a submarine.

Laugh, Cry, Reflect

I held my speed to exactly 25, but the headlights still loomed, making the hairs on my neck rise.

An Eagle River trooper told me he once stopped an elderly man who had a creative excuse. "I'm listening to the Book of Mark because I want to memorize it for church and recite parts of it. I got so involved I wasn't paying attention to the speedometer." He'd gotten off with a warning, and the officer heard later that the man did do an impressive recitation. I fumbled around in the middle console hoping to pull out a religious CD, but wouldn't you know it, I ended up with Cher's *Just Like Jesse James*.

How about using the excuse of a possessed car? A speeder swore to the Eagle River officer that something had taken over her car and even though she'd tried to brake, she couldn't stop the vehicle. Car demons? Hmmm. Would my officer believe that story?

Another speeder said he was going too fast because they were camping and needed hot dog buns. Those buns ended up costing hundreds of dollars.

Maybe I could pick the soppiest excuse I've ever heard. After one woman was pulled over, she poured half her water bottle onto her lap. When the

~ 18 ~

officer peered in, she explained she had a bladder problem. *He let her go!* Hmm, I had a water bottle on the floor of the passenger side. I struggled, and finally reached over far enough to grab it. Drat, it was empty.

When the red lights flashed, my stomach dropped to my toes. I pulled over and shut the car off. My chest felt like it was being torpedoed by submarines. An elderly friend had recently been pulled over for doing 75. She'd been so scared she'd pressed her hands on her chest, sure she was having a heart attack. The officer calmed her down and gently sent her along her way. Would that work for me?

An officer I didn't recognize approached my car. I lowered my window.

"May I see your license?"

I fumbled through all the cards in my wallet before I finally landed on it.

"You were weaving a bit back there," the officer said. "What was that all about?"

I didn't want to say I was rifling through my CDs looking for something religious and reaching for my water bottle hoping to find a perfect excuse.

Instead, I stammered, "I, uh, was thinking about hot dog buns and bladder problems."

He frowned at me. "Have you been drinking?"

"No!"

"I clocked you at 35 in a 25 zone."

I nearly corrected him and confessed that I was doing 37.

"So what's the reason for your speed?"

"I . . . I can't think of a thing."

An urgent voice on the squad car's radio talked in code. The officer listened, then quickly said, "I'm letting you off with a warning this time, but watch the speed." Seconds later, siren blaring, he sped off.

I sat a minute, then finally pulled onto the road, setting the cruise for the speed limit. I was going to go nice and slow, at least until I dreamed up the perfect excuse.

Links of Love

The True Tale of the Ugliest Quilt Ever

The ugliest quilt ever

A friend of mine became excited about a new quilt pattern called "Jelly Roll Race." Colors and prints are randomly pieced together and can result in an attractive surprise. Anticipating a pleasing work of art, she eagerly gathered the supplies. She measured, cut strips, then sewed all the strips together end to end. Still more hours were required to put it together and add fleece on the back. Finally she stood back to look. U-gly!

She had made the ugliest quilt imaginable. Lacking design, the haphazard colors and patterns were far from a pleasing work of art. After all the hours she'd put in, she wanted to find a remedy. Maybe an interesting array of diamond-shaped appliqués would help. She got to work. She stepped back to look. Impossible.

The quilt was even uglier. The appliqués looked misplaced and had added a busyness to the random pattern. They seemed more like patches which were sewn on to cover up mistakes. My friend felt defeated, but since she'd invested even more time on the quilt, she determinedly persisted.

She remembered admiring a quilt that had rickrack meandering around on the top. Robin's egg blue might add interest. She bought the rickrack and spent a few more hours sewing. Finally, she stepped back to look. Unbelievable. She'd made the quilt even uglier. It could be the ugliest quilt in existence.

She hid the quilt in the back of her closet.

Meanwhile, an older acquaintance became hospitalized. The gentleman complained about being cold. My friend jokingly told him she had a warm quilt and he was welcome to it as long as he didn't tell anyone who had made it. Sheepishly, she brought it to him. She wrapped it around his shoulders. He smiled, pulled it tight to his chest, and clasped her hand in thanks.

When the gentleman was transferred to an assisted living center, the quilt went with him. When he returned to the hospital again, so did the quilt.

It makes me wonder. Did its warmth remind him of when he was a child and his mother would pull up a homemade quilt and tuck him in at night? Or did it bring to mind his own family and the times he'd snuggled with his children, his loving wife looking on?

Maybe the quilt's appliquéd patches made him recall an earlier time in his life when his days were full, abounding with purposeful and productive activities. It's possible the rickrack resembling long stretches of roads brought to mind a time in his life when he could take off after work and drive for the sheer joy of the journey. Or it might not have been any of these things. The quilt might simply have brought him comfort because he knew that a friend had spent many hours making it and then had shared it with him.

Sadly, the gentleman passed away. My friend attended the funeral. Before the attendant closed the casket, he reached down by the gentleman's feet and pulled something up. Something with haphazard colors and meandering rickrack. Something with misplaced patches and fleece worn thin from use. Something that had brought comfort to a dying man.

It's a beautiful story, this true tale of the ugliest quilt ever.

Drawing on the Strength
of Mothers Before Me

Wooden bracelet with family photos

$\mathcal{M}$y aunts presented me with a special gift, a bracelet with wooden panels bearing photos of my mother Marcia, grandmother Caroline, great-grandmother Bertha, and great-great-grandmother Mekka. To the right of my mother is a photo of me. It's followed by my two daughters. The bracelet is brown, the color of roasted coffee, a love we all share.

I stare at the photo of my mother showing her as a zestful young woman. So much of who I am is a result of how she raised me, encouraged me, what she said and didn't say, and especially how she lived her life. That photo evokes memories of my adolescence when she and I danced the polka to *Roll out the Barrel*, and I learned one of the greatest lessons, to make the most of every day of your life.

Next to Mom on the bracelet is Grandma Caroline, whose quick sense of humor brought lightness to hard times. She and her husband (who once had to hock his watch for gas money) struggled to eke out a living on their Wisconsin farm. Grandma was a good money manager and her and my grandpa's hard work eventually allowed them to retire and enjoy traveling and a few luxuries. Grandma was a baker of wonderful poppyseed cakes, a helpmate to her husband, and a woman of integrity and strong faith. I study the bracelet and reflect. Which of her genes do I carry?

Next to her is my great-grandmother Bertha, who also married a farmer just managing to scrape by. When a pompous male relative bragged that he didn't have to work with his hands like they did, that he used his head instead, this sharp-witted woman replied, "Use your head? Oh, just like the chickens pecking in the dirt."

I look at the photo of my great-great-grandmother Mekka and wish I could introduce myself. "Hello, I'm the daughter of Marcia, who's the daughter of Caroline, who's the daughter of Bertha, your daughter. Let's brew up some of that coffee we Norwegians love and sit down and catch up."

The final photo is to the right of my picture and shows my two daughters, bright-eyed and smiling. Someday I hope they pour themselves a cup of coffee and reflect on these womanly links.

Stitching a Life Together

*W*hile cleaning out a storage closet, I pulled out two blue chambray shirts, one extra-large, one medium. I'd purchased them as a Valentine's gift over twenty years ago for my husband and me. I'd read a romance novel and chambray was the shirt of choice for the muscular, wild, and rugged cowboy. I'm not sure if I told my husband about the novel or my romantic imaginings, but either way, the gesture was lost and the shirts barely worn.

I study the baby-blue shirts. I'd been so naïve back then. I didn't yet understand that our connectedness wouldn't come from wearing matching shirts, but from years of juggling careers with family and chores. We were a perfectly matched pair when one was paying bills and the other was in charge of laundry; one fixing the overflowing toilet, the other on hold for hours with the computer technician; one cooking dinner and the other monitoring homework.

By the time we had older children, we had choreographed who slept with one eye open when the kids were sick and who kept track if they made curfew. Frank had the stomach to clean up vomit; I was in charge of dog waste. Not necessarily romantic, but we were in sync.

We knew the importance of being on the same page when it came to disciplining the kids, and they knew not to ask if the other parent had already said "No." We haven't done quite as well with our dog, however. Josie knows that if one of us doesn't give her a belly rub or treat, the other probably will.

Bonding happens as much from surviving the rough times as the good ones. Issues with children, finances, stresses at work, aging parents, illnesses and loss of loved ones can be overcome with a partner's support. Who cares about matching outfits when you find a mate who knows just where your stressed muscles need massaging, or just the right words to lift your spirits.

I now know the importance of simple gestures such as bringing me home a McDonald's coffee with one cream.

Romantic thrills don't need to come from camping overnight under the Wyoming sky. They can come from a dazzling snowfall that allows us to make fresh tracks from the cabin to the woods and lake. Or from watching an animated dog try to contain her excitement when we go through the drive-up window knowing she'll get the last bit of our ice cream cones.

I know his tennis game improves the longer he plays; he knows after an hour mine declines. (We both take advantage of that knowledge.) I know he needs time in his man cave with a large screen TV; he knows I need reading and writing time.

We're a perfect match when I shop for the bread dough, pecans, and syrup, and he bakes his famous cinnamon rolls so our kids and grandkids can awaken to the cinnamon smell they associate with home.

Romance isn't symbolized by matching shirts, but by a beloved thread-bare recliner meant for one but sometimes utilized by two plus a wiggly dog.

Matching shirts can't compare with standing side by side smiling as our grown children banter over who won at cards or who caught the smallest perch. Together we comment on how our grandson has my face shape and my husband's lips. More importantly, we melt as he crawls to our out-stretched arms.

Ironically, this Christmas we ended up receiving matching hunter-green vests. Someday we may happen to both wear them. We probably won't notice. We'll be too busy watching our children zigzag away at their dreams and reveling as our grandchildren button-hole their way into our hearts. Identical shirts aren't needed to stitch a life together.

She Has My Eyes

$\mathcal{M}$y three-and-a-half-year-old granddaughter looked across the dinner table studying my face. "Grammy, you have blue eyes."

"Yes," I said, "and they're the exact same ice-blue color as yours."

Our common eye color isn't due to genetics, but as in many step-families, Vanessa and I share something much more important than DNA.

Earlier that day, she had asked if I would take her to the fairy forest near our family cabin. We explored under the delicate tree canopy, among the sphagnum moss and plants that look like soft, miniature pine trees, and sure enough, we found evidence—a fairy's red stop sign. (Botanists would call it a fungus, *hygrophorus puniceus*, but we knew what it really was.)

Next we picked a daisy bouquet, and I taught her the classic "He loves me, he loves me not" daisy chant. We plucked petal by petal. Seeing we were going to end with "He loves me not," I showed her how to pluck two petals at once, an old family trick.

I let her climb to the top of a boulder and guarded her as she leapt off like Bat Woman. "Grammy," she finally said, "I'm tired. Will you give me a piggyback ride?"

"All the way home, just like this little piggy?"

"Oh, yes, Grammy."

Once home, Vanessa picked out our treasured book of the week and knew I'd abandon dinner preparations to read it to her. Our favorite page tells about a girl who has to change her baby sister's dirty diaper. The girl exclaims, "Pee-yoo!" and we hold our noses, make a scrunchy face, look at each other, blue eyes to blue eyes, and together chant, "Pee-yoo!"

Giggle, laugh, snort, hiccup.

Someday the family might sit around talking about how Vanessa has the exact same nose/hairline/body shape/jaw as so-and-so. My name won't be mentioned, but I won't care. My thoughts will be elsewhere. Does she still remember finding a fairy's stop sign? Will she want me to come to her gymnastic class and spot her as she leaps, spins, and twirls? And when she's in the school comedy, delivering her clever lines, will I laugh so loud I hiccup?

No, we don't share the same genetics. We share a whole lot more.

Mother and Daughter

$\mathcal{M}$y mother's and my roles switched when she dislocated a shoulder, fractured her sacrum, started experiencing severe breathing problems, and nearly died. I was now the caregiver, which included washing and setting her hair.

As a young child, my mother set my hair in pink spongy curlers for special occasions. She, in turn, would ask me to brush her hair. My strokes were fumbling yet heartfelt, much like the homemade Mother's Day cards that always had a purple, wild wood violet inside—wilted of course.

As an older child, my brush strokes were stronger but impatient. At 15, with my hair ironed and squirted with a lightener to make it blonder, the last thing I wanted to do was fuss with my mother's hair. On the rare occasion that I did, my strokes were clipped.

As a busy young mother in my twenties and thirties, I don't remember ever sitting down to brush my mother's hair. All those wasted years when I might have had a private moment, a chance to ask advice or hear what was in her heart.

My brother's call broke into my thoughts. He and I were discussing our worries about Mom's health when feeble steps approached. I felt an unsteady hand pull a brush through my hair. A gentle stroke ran down its length. Patiently, Mom raised her arm again and again.

My shoulders eased. My heart lifted. An overpowering outpouring of love washed over me. I couldn't speak. Mother and daughter. We've come full circle.

A Time to Mourn and a Time to Dance

I offered my mother a sip of the hospital's coffee then wiped her chin when it dribbled down. The woman who had first wiped my milk-dribbled chin now depended on me to wipe hers.

She was suffering and I knew it was wrong of me, but my thoughts became selfish. *How will I ever live without her? She was always there when I needed advice or help. What would I do without this woman who knew my every fault, yet still loved me?*

Mom took another sip of coffee and looked at me. Her eyes moistened. Was she remembering something from my past, maybe one of the episodes she'd often told me about? I was the baby who loved to cuddle, the toddler who played in the fresh road tar ruining her church dress, and the adolescent who sassed off. I stroked her hand, bruised and covered by skin as thin as onion peels. She closed her eyes and rested.

Inside this failing body was the woman who sent me to the store for Raleigh cigarettes, letting me keep a nickel for myself; the animal lover who would even carry bugs outside rather than kill them; the woman who enjoyed playing cards, having coffee with friends, reading Agatha Christie mysteries and Emily Dickinson poetry; who introduced me to writers like Leon Uris and James Michener; who rode a motorcycle one summer before deciding it was too unsafe; who survived the death of her first husband at an early age and continued on.

Mom had worn crimson lipstick on special occasions and had loved to dance. I remember attending a wedding with a polka band and she'd reached out for my hand. We'd twirled around, yee-hawing with unleashed joy.

The next time I returned to her hospital bed, she was hooked up to multiple tubes. I stroked her fragile skin. "I love you, Mom. You are a marvelous mother. I'm so lucky to have you."

She squeezed my hand. "When the pain gets too bad, I try to remember something wonderful, like walking the dog in the blooming desert. Or I think of my children. The best thing that ever happened to me was to have you kids."

My husband walked to Mom's bedside. Her eyes closed. "Go to sleep, Marcia," he said tenderly. "Don't fight it."

She nodded.

The following morning we were called to her bedside for the last time. My eyes brimmed with tears as the family gathered, held hands, and her chest rose for the last time. How will we ever get through this?

Then I remembered. In karate, my instructor once had us do an exercise where we had to push over a weighted bag. I tried and tried without success. He finally said, "Amy, you have to look beyond the bag. Focus past it." I stood close this time, looked past the bag, and pushed. It went right over.

Now I knew what I had to do. I would look beyond this hospital bed, beyond my mother's pain, to a place filled with light and warmth and God's love, a place where she can walk her dog and see the Arizona desert in bloom, a place where she can greet loved ones who have gone before, and wait for those who will follow. In this place, she and I will once again kick up our heels and dance.

The Best Gift

*T*he best gift we can give does not always need to be wrapped. It may be a gift we don't even realize we've given until much later.

I walked into the funeral home for my beloved step-father's visitation. He'd married my mother a few years after my father died, when I was in my late twenties. Needing to work up courage before I viewed his body, I read the cards on the potted flowers and vases. The sheer volume proved what I'd known, that Harold had been a true friend and generous neighbor, always ready to share anything, from his garden tools to a cup of coffee.

The family flower spray included the word *Grandfather*. Besides taking an interest in his biological grandchildren, Harold became close to Frank's and my children, especially Heidi, who lived nearby. Harold helped her and her husband search want ads for jobs and apartments. He had a gentle way of offering advice which they often took.

The word *Husband* on Harold's spray made me recall what a devoted partner and caregiver he'd been to my mother. He kept meticulous records of her medications and appointments. His love for her kept her going through long illnesses. Harold's wish was to die on the one-year anniversary of her death and he only missed it by a few days.

I shifted my focus to another spray of flowers with the word *Father*. It must have been hard to move into the house another man had built. Only my youngest sister was still living at home, but Harold once told me how stressful it was for him to be at family gatherings because he wasn't sure we wanted him there. Oh, how I wish I could have those times back. I would have welcomed him with open arms.

As people started to enter, I knew this was my last chance to share a private moment with Harold. I caught sight of a frame on the end of the casket. I walked over to take a look. Inside was a picture of me and a column I'd written, back when I used the byline Emily Braatz. Entitled "Human Fathers Mirror Nature," it was a Father's Day piece in which I'd compared my biological father to a prairie dog always on alert. I wrote, "My family wasn't the type to say I love you, and my father and I never had a chance to exchange those precious words." It went on to say I was fortunate enough to acquire a wonderful step-father, "one who is as steadfast and devoted to my mother as the gander standing by his mate's side, protecting her from danger. Harold and I grow closer every time we're together." It ended with, "I hope you get the opportunity to spend time with your father, biological or otherwise, and that you have the chance to tell him 'I love you.'"

A pink sticky note on the upper right-hand side of the frame caught my eye. I recognized Harold's neat handwriting. The note said: "This framed article is to be placed on my casket. This is the best gift that I have ever received."

I choked with emotion, barely able to breathe. I searched my mind, recalling giving Harold a copy of that column years ago.

Harold's son joined me. "I found this with his important papers," he said. "It must have meant a great deal to Dad." I opened my arms, gave him a hug, and he gave me one in return.

The frame with the sticky note sits on my office shelf. It reminds me of how a person can bring joy through simple expressions of love and acceptance. We just have to open our arms.

A Slice of Life
By Emily Braatz

Human fathers mirror nature

In nature, as in life, fathers come in all varieties. There's the tom turkey who's out to get as many hens as he can...

[Handwritten note on pink card:] This framed article is to be placed on my casket. This is best gift that I have ever recieved

My stepfather wanted one of my columns placed on his casket.

Hey, Teach!

What I've Learned

I was an elementary teacher for over 30 years. I'm not sure how much I taught, but I know I learned a lot. Here's a sample.

- When a child starts running for the bathroom, don't delay him by asking what's wrong.

- There are certain words (ball, screw, or nuts) that will send fourth graders rolling in the aisle.

- Don't wear white to school, especially when hurrying around a corner carrying coffee.

- Do not assume that when a coworker complains about bad behavior during a field trip, she means the students. She may mean the chaperones.

- Don't let a birthday boy or girl serve red fruit punch on the day class pictures are taken.

- There is no point in asking kids to use glitter sparingly.

- Don't ask fourth graders to bring firewood on Pioneer Day without also bringing a pickup to haul all of it away.

- If a student says he's feeling sick on the bus, don't pause to ask questions. Grab the garbage pail, then stand back.

- Don't mention that the class frog is almost out of worms on a day when it has rained unless you have a big worm container.

- If a child says it looks like you have a black eye, it's time to check your makeup.

- If several kids ask to use the bathroom, it's time to change the activity.

- Don't look under desktops if you want to have an appetite at lunch.

- Bring tissue to patriotic assemblies where the students sing "America."

- Don't trust the eye test results of a girl who's envious of a best friend's new purple glasses.

- On April Fool's Day, skip the calendar lesson and pray no one remembers.

- For all the trouble special days and field trips are, they are also what kids remember.

- Comfortable shoes are much more important than style.

- Students will do better if they know you care about them.

- School lunch is sometimes the best meal a child has that day.

- Watching butterflies hatch out of cocoons is exciting, but watching the face of a child seeing it for the first time is even more fun.

- Kids love Halloween, even more than Christmas.

- The child who gives you the most grief is, on the last day of school, most likely to give the longest hug.

- Don't assume that the child continually taking off her new glasses doesn't like them. She might be wanting to "save them so she doesn't use them up."

- Kids are more impressed with my rusty karate moves than with my diplomas.

- Ponce de Leon didn't have to look halfway around the world for the Fountain of Youth. Working with kids keeps a person young.

The lessons I've taught over the years are numerous, but one thing's for sure. I've learned every bit as much as the kids.

My Smelly Reputation

*T*he janitor, spray can in hand, looked around my fourth-grade classroom. "Did a snake escape and die in some corner?"

"No, I don't think so." I breathed through my mouth to avoid the smell. A girl had recently brought in a grass snake in an uncovered container. As the reptile slithered its way up the side of the bowl, I told her she'd have to take it out to the school garden. I was called to the office, and I'm pretty sure the snake made it outside. Ninety percent sure, anyway.

The janitor left to see if he had more deodorizer. I checked the fish tank, the guinea pig cage, the terrarium, and the worms we were collecting for Froglegs, the aquatic frog. Nothing smelly here.

Two teachers, one pinching her nose shut, stood outside my door shaking their heads. I heard, "It's coming from her room again."

"I'm probably known as Mrs. Yuck," I muttered, still trying to find the offensive smell. Speaking of yuck, where is that present the art teacher gave me? I searched a cupboard for the bright red box. She'd brought it in one morning and said, "Now, don't take this wrong, but you're the only person I know who will appreciate this." I'd opened the cover and gently pulled back red tissue paper to find the complete skeleton of a mouse that had been caught in a trap. It showed the skull, the vertebrae, and most fascinating of all, the delicate tail bone. I was delighted and used it as a reward after students finished their assignment.

Still sniffing, I opened another cupboard and found the nest a student had brought in. It contained the skeletons of four baby birds. After discussing vertebrate systems, the class and I made predictions as to what had happened. Then I'd told a few stories about the classroom finches I'd had years ago. They'd hatched only one egg, but I'll always remember that tiny, perfectly formed baby. I took a whiff. Nope, not coming from the bird's nest.

Students had begun filing in and now the *Pee-yoo*'s and *Ooo-eee*'s started in chorus. "What's that smell?" several students asked.

"I'm not sure," I began, "but would everyone please check their desks?"

I noticed a girl in the last row open and then quickly close hers shut. I walked closer. The smell was getting stronger. "It's okay, Sweetie. Tell me."

"Remember Thursday when I asked you if we could have show-and-tell on Friday and you said yes but then we never had it?"

I did vaguely remember an unexpected visitor during show-and-tell time. "Go ahead and open your desk." I drew in a deep breath and held it. Lying on top of her science book was a Ziploc bag filled with mush. "What is that?"

A flush creeping across her cheeks, she whispered, "A blue gill. At least it was a blue gill."

Fourth graders chuckled.

The girl tilted her head back and turned accusatory eyes at me. "Remember how you said if someone brought one in, we'd dissect it and find its swim bladder?"

"Yes, do you think you might have told me you'd brought in a fish so I could have made sure you got to show it?"

The little girl gave a small nod then quickly brightened. "Don't worry. I'll catch you another one."

Yes, I think, it's definitely time to clean up my act. Later that day, I'd just begun the science lesson when I overheard a teacher's voice in the hall. "*Ewww*, you must be looking for Mrs. L., room 149."

A minute later a boy appeared at my desk to present me with a bag of owl pellets. I tried to control my excitement. "Thank you." I pulled one out. "Wow! Gather around, class. This is awesome!" I broke one apart. "A mouse skull! How cool is that? This was probably spit up by a great horned owl. Owls' digestive systems can't handle fur and bones, so they regurgitate these pellets. Let's break open another. We might find snake skin or even a bit of skunk fur."

Ah, I decided, rolling up my sleeves, cleaning up my reputation can wait until next year.

Back in the Good Ol' Days

*W*ell, I finally did it. I used those dreaded words that instantly categorize a person as over the hill. They came out of my mouth before I could stop them. They made me cringe, groan, and wrinkle my already wrinkled forehead. The words were, *"Back in my day."*

In my defense, I didn't have much of a choice. When I mentioned a typewriter, my students frowned in puzzlement, so I explained. I found myself wondering what my students will tell their children about their good ol' days. Will they bemoan the fact that cell phones in their day didn't have the features their grandchildren's latest technology has?

The one thing I've found that crosses all time-lines is playing games. On Pioneer Day, my classroom vibrated with excited laughter while students played "Drop the Clothespin into the Jar." They twirled one another around for "Pin the Tail on the Donkey," just as I did during my childhood birthday parties. Outside, the laughter kept coming during "Leapfrog," "Duck, Duck, Goose" and wheelbarrow races. Children squealed while playing "Crack the Whip" and giggled while stepping into a feed sack and hopping to the finish line. I thought of the George Bernard Shaw quotation: "We don't stop playing because we grow old; we grow old because we stop playing."

I joined the kids and stepped into a feed sack myself. *Boing, boing, boing.* It was as much fun as ever. Maybe I'm not over the hill after all.

More Lessons I've Learned

Every year, my students teach me new lessons. Here's a sample.

- If I eat a liverwurst and onion sandwich for lunch, my students are sure to say something.

- Giving kids choices and ownership in the classroom makes for a smoother year.

- The public library, the dollar store, and rummage sales are great places to get school materials.

- I can never have too much vinegar and baking soda when it comes time to let students do volcano experiments.

- Some of the art pieces my fourth-graders have done are every bit as good as those sold at art studios, and I'd love to display them in my home.

- Memorizing facts is far less important than learning where to find them.

- When nine-year-old boys huddle together looking at a *National Geographic*, they're not reading the articles.

- Recess isn't just for the students.

- Students don't realize how much time my coworkers and I spend thinking about them, and we teachers probably don't realize how much our students think about us.

- When I take moments out for myself, I'm a better teacher.

- If kids spent as much time on homework as they do with TV and other screens, they'd earn straight A's.

- Meetings or useless paperwork that takes a teacher's time and energy ends up hurting the students.

- If I expect a lot from my students, I'm much more apt to get it.

- Asking a veteran teacher for advice is much more helpful than educational textbooks.

- Beginning band instructors deserve a special place in heaven.

- One of the nicest gifts I can receive from a parent or student is a heartfelt thank-you card.

- Kids who know how to get along with one another are more likely to be successful than those with only a high IQ.

- If I'm having fun teaching a lesson, chances are the students are having fun learning it.

- The moment when the light goes on is as thrilling for me as it is for the student.

- Instead of saying a story needs to be five pages, if I say it can't be more than five pages, I'll have students begging to be allowed to write ten or fifteen.

- There are no dumb questions, but "Is it time for recess yet?" is sure to raise my hackles.

- Spending more money on schools may not be the best way to spend less on prisons, but it sure is a great start.

- Watching a male and female dog on the playground is far more interesting than learning the parts of the reproductive system.

- When I lose my temper, I lose respect.

- Letting students know I make mistakes and learn from them is a valuable lesson.

- Making students stay in from recess and write sentences implies that writing is a punishment, and I don't do it anymore.

- It takes more than one adult to raise a child, but just one adult can make all the difference.

- Every student excels at something. It's my job to help the students discover their talents.

Teaching has its downfalls, but it's rarely boring. As long as I'm teaching, I'm sure to learn lessons.

Revelations

Homeless Experience Prompts Understanding

After finishing a lunch at a nice restaurant, my family and I pulled out of the parking lot. I spotted a long-haired, disheveled man and guessed he was homeless. Had he brought his troubles on himself, or been a victim of circumstances? As I wondered, he staggered along the sidewalk then fell down in the grass and vomited. A van driver pulled into the restaurant parking lot, stopped, pointed, then turned to his passenger and laughed.

Life is filled with moments of indecision, and for me, this was one of them. Do I snarl at the laugher, help the man, or call the police? I did nothing.

The image stayed with me, though, and when I had the chance, I talked it over with a police officer friend. He said circumstances vary but generally calling the police is the best option. The police will make sure there isn't a warrant out and will advise the person about local resources.

I wish the mocker who laughed could have joined my friend's twelve-year-old son, Adam, who spent an April night in a cardboard box to support the homeless. He, three other Boy Scouts, and a leader slept outside in the parking lot of a Walmart. They connected their boxes with duct tape for added warmth against the 30-degree temperature. The boys were allowed to bring only those supplies they were willing to carry all day long, as homeless people have to do. Adam brought a pillow, blanket, flashlight, book to help pass the time, backpack to tote his items, a can of soup for the planned Hobo Stew, eating utensils, and $5.00 to help with food expenses.

Friday night the Salvation Army truck, equipped with a propane stove, warmed up the stew. Spirits were still high until night descended. Using a port-a-potty and sleeping on the cold ground were cruel realities. At 3:15 Adam awoke, failed to get comfortable, and lay awake the rest of the night.

In the morning, he and the troop visited with people about their experience and passed out Salvation Army flyers suggesting donations of clothing, toiletries, and canned food.

A homeless man came to talk to the boys telling how much of his time is spent planning where he's going to sleep, where he'll find food, and how to stay warm. He told Adam a lot of homeless people end up stealing and many drink too much.

Twenty-two hours after arriving at his cardboard box, Adam returned home to his cozy bed, his indoor plumbing, his family, and his life. I think it was a great service project. Adam is proud he helped the cause and has a renewed sense of gratitude. I doubt he'd ever stick his head out of a car window, point at a homeless person, and laugh.

My Secret to Weight Loss

Josie, the best personal trainer

*D*o you want to increase your exercising and maybe lose a few pounds? Forget joining the gym. I have the solution. Get a puppy!

After getting Josie, a silky black Cockapoo, my husband and I have been more active than ever. She's an ideal personal trainer.

Before the snow fell, her jumping on my bike tire was all the motivation I needed to don my helmet. She contentedly sat in her special basket and took in the scenery. Some days I was tempted to do less than our usual six miles, but I kept moving knowing Josie would miss sniffing the pig farm, barking at the guinea hens, and listening to the chorus at the frog pond.

During the warm fall days, I encouraged her to play in the lake water. Of course, that meant I had to splash around, too. By next summer, she may have me swimming laps.

I love to walk along the river or in the woods on bright days, but dreary weather can make me lazy. No longer. All my personal trainer needs to do is stand by the door and look up at me pleadingly with her brown eyes. I hurry into my hiking boots.

Josie loves playing soccer with a small beach ball and she's very good at it, darting past me as she bats the ball with her front paws, her head tucked in making it hard for me to sweep it away with my foot. The aerobic exercise not only strengthens lungs and heart, but lowers my cholesterol, increases muscle strength, and is just plain fun.

When it's too cold to be outdoors, we have a favorite search game, Hide and Seek. I hide behind a chair or door, call out, "Find me," and she sniffs me out, wagging her tail and wiggling when she's successful. She also likes to show off one of her best tricks. She pulls a stuffed toy named Big Mean Kitty around in a little red wagon. I ask you, who needs to raid the fridge and eat mindlessly when instead you can watch a puppy at play?

Besides getting so much exercise, I'm saving calories. With an active puppy, I don't take time to bake fattening desserts like cookies. So how much weight have I lost, you ask? Only two pounds, but hey, it's a start. My personal trainer will tell you that a pet is not only good for exercising the body, it's good for warming the heart.

P.S. My mum doesn't know I'm adding a P.S. (actually she doesn't even know I can write), but I just wanted to add that if you happen to see her around town, please put in a good word for me. It seems only fair that Mum ought to increase my daily allowance of doggie treats. After all, personal trainers don't come cheap. And don't let her fool you. She isn't a baker and wouldn't have made cookies even if I weren't nagging her for a walk.

Wag, Wag,

Josie

The Magical Little Cabin in the Woods

A remote getaway place, such as a cabin in the woods, can be magical for you and your family. It is in our tiny cabin, among the trees and along the lake, that our friends and family prefer to come together to celebrate, go on adventures, and build memories.

My daughter and I were skiing in Land O' Lakes, Wisconsin, when she commented that if we hadn't planned this cabin trip, she wouldn't have come to visit us in our home. Our home in the city, I mused, where we're interrupted with phone calls, meetings, and the internet. When we're at our little cabin in the woods, we concentrate on one another-- pure magic.

During our cabin stays, family or friends need to bunk close together, but that means we also plan together. This morning should we ski or snowshoe? How about either homemade chili or fresh fish for lunch? Afterward do we want to ice fish or drive to see the waterfalls?

Each season holds its own magic. Last winter, we discovered a waterfall encased in an ice cave. Another wintery day we skied through the woods and spotted a face appearing to be a mix between a fox and a teddy bear, our first glimpse of a fisher. One memorable Christmas morning, our family skied in the Sylvania wilderness, making the first tracks through fresh snow. We ended that day dining at one of our favorite restaurants, then relaxing with a movie.

Memories of spring's magic include one morning when five otters splashed and romped along the lake's shoreline. One gave chase and soon all were in a wrestling match.

Summer holds memories of outdoor fish fries, waterskiing, kayaking, and swimming in the lake. Playing a game I call Splish-splash with the youngest grandchildren tops the list. Snorkeling with the older ones in hopes of seeing a school of fish or a turtle is a close second.

Fall at the cabin, when the light plays off the rich colors, is my favorite season for outdoor photography. It's also the best time to take sunlit rides through the countryside on roads edged with maples, or boat on the lake where the golden hues of birch and maple reflect in the still water. Fall is often the time we tackle remodeling projects or chores such as raking. Even jobs can be fun at the cabin.

What is magical about our little cabin in the woods? Family and friends have a shared history here. It's where my husband and I honeymooned, where relatives celebrated their 50th anniversary, and where we've had family reunions. The annual Mens' Weekend includes snowmobiling and playing cards until the wee hours of the morning. The Children's Weekend includes nature walks and keeping alive traditions such as harvesting winter-green leaves to brew tea.

How can four log walls hold such power? It's not the walls, of course, but the foundation of family; the mortar of wanting to share each other's lives, the seasoned logs of an enduring future. There's no place like our little cabin in the woods.

Motherhood, the Corporate World

I was grabbing a quick lunch at a fast-food restaurant when a family walked in. The grandmother held the door while the mother, carrying a baby, encouraged a little girl clinging to her knee to go on ahead. They stood in line a while. The baby fussed and Mom efficiently pulled a bottle out of the diaper bag, expertly snapping off the lid. Grandma was giving the food order when the little girl raced toward the exit. Not missing a beat, the mom shifted so she held baby and bottle in one hand, grabbing the toddler with the other.

Mom directed the family to the table next to mine. She handed the baby to Grandma then whisked a highchair to the table and had the little girl strapped in within seconds. She pulled a burger out of the bag.

"Don't lick the tray, Sarah," Mom said. "I've almost got this cut up. No, no! Young ladies do not stick their fingers in their nose. Here," she said kissing the little girl's forehead, "I have this all set for you." She moved aside allowing me to see the neat arrangement of bun, burger, and straw inserted in milk carton.

"But I wanted a bun-dog," the girl said.

"You can have a hot dog for supper," Mom said.

The baby wailed. "She likes to be patted hard on the back while she's burped," Mom directed Grandma.

Grandma patted harder.

"Catsup, Mommy," the little girl said. "I do myself."

"No, I'll do it."

But Sarah had already started ripping the small packet open. Catsup squirted onto the girl's white shirt. "Oh, no!" the girl wailed.

"Don't worry," the mom said in a surprisingly calm voice. Turning to Grandma, she said, "I found a new presoak and it works like magic." Mom sniffed. She sniffed again. "Oops, I think Daniel needs a diaper change."

When Mom returned from the bathroom with Daniel, Sarah said, "Mommy, I have to go potty, too. I have to go now!"

Mom handed Daniel back to Grandma, whipped Sarah out of the highchair, and sprinted away as smoothly as an Olympic runner.

Whew! I was exhausted just watching. I had finished my salad when the mom returned. The girl took one bite of her hamburger. "I'm done," she said, pushing it aside. She bent over a toy.

"I've been wanting to ask," the grandma began. "How did your job interview go?"

The mom shrugged. "I doubt I'll get it. I'm not qualified for the corporate world. They're looking for someone who can handle stress, anticipates others' needs, and can multitask. What experience have I had to prepare me for that?"

What indeed?

Mates' Preferences Duel while Love Prevails

I'm drawn to the magazine ads showing kitchens that cater to contrasting personalities. One example is "High Fashion Marries High Tech," which features an elegant woman in a flowing dress standing beside a computer nerd.

It makes me think about couples I know who are clearly very different from one another. The wife enjoys dining on a fresh shrimp salad with mango dressing served on a dainty china rose plate while her husband likes beer and brats. She saves up for spa treatments; he spends money to attend tractor pulls, car races, and demolition derbies.

A female friend dreams of owning a horse ranch in the rolling hills of Colorado where she can steeplechase her thoroughbred over streams and fences. Her mate wants a low-maintenance condo in the city where he doesn't have to worry about mowing, trimming, or raking.

A woman I know admires fine art pieces, including sculptures and original oils, whereas her husband wants to set a full-size, lifelike bear and cougar mount in their living room. She ordered a new Queen Anne's clawfoot chintz chair, and he fought to keep his comfy old recliner. She prefers walking the beach wearing a classy swimsuit with flowing overskirt in yellow and blue swirls, and he likes deserted beaches where he can skinny-dip. How do they get along? I just don't get it.

How does someone who dreams about getting that 30-point buck coexist with a mate who longs for new French provincial furniture?

One mate wants to vacation in the Cayman Islands, while the other wants to fish walleye in Canada. One enjoys romantic sensual movies like *Under the Tuscan Sun*, while the other prefers rip-'em-up action thrillers. One prefers dinner music, the other wants to listen to the news. One loves to read the morning paper on the sun porch; the other reads on the toilet. How can such diverse personalities coexist?

Do you know of people who would find hunting for a great bargain just as exciting as their mates would find hunting for grizzlies? How about the spouse who diets only to find no change, married to a person who can shed 10 pounds by simply sneezing? One partner enjoys gazing upon fresh flowers arranged in a crystal vase, the other catching sight of darting trout in a crystal-clear stream.

I'm jubilant after figuring out a computer problem, whereas my husband's mood soars if he can squeeze all the suitcases in the car. I prefer sipping a glass of Chablis while soaking in the hot tub at sunset, whereas my mate enjoys sitting in a turkey blind with a hot cup of coffee at sunrise. How do such dueling personalities get along? I truly have no idea.

Thanks to my husband, Frank, for his contributions to this column. He's off now to sit in the turkey blind, and I, well, I have the Chablis chilling.

People Break Stereotypes in Surprising Ways

I'm constantly surprised by people.

I love watching the woman in heels and a flowery dress bypass the sedans and ride away on her moped. A tattooed, leather-clad guy in boots passed up the Harleys and drove away in a station wagon. A young man with orange-moussed hair and a dozen earrings tenderly held his sister's hand while they crossed the street.

A male relative likes to pretend to be tough, cussing with the guys, drinking hard and talking rough, but I once caught him patiently training a chipmunk to come eat sunflower seeds out of his hand.

I've listened to a man scoff that he never wanted children, then watched as he melted with pure joy when he held his newborn. I know a great-grandma who has never held a crocheting needle, preferring to gentle spirited horses instead. And I've heard of a hunter who climbs into his tree stand not to shoot

Revelations

but to write poetry. People are amazingly complex and just when we think we've got them figured out, we discover a deeper layer.

One story of how people break the mold stands out from all the rest. A friend stopped at a place where a young man was selling chain saw art. She looked over the various sculptures then sought out the young man for help. "Are you one of the artists?"

"No," the young man mumbled.

"What kind of wood is this bear made from?" my friend asked.

"Don't know," the young man replied, then walked away.

My friend sighed. She knew the type well—surly teenager, probably one concerned with buying another skateboard. She chose her bear and silently handed the young man a check. He carried the same bear to her car and gently lowered it into the trunk. He looked at it a moment, moving the car blanket around its body as someone would tuck in a child at bedtime. "His name," the young man whispered to my friend, "is Fluffy."

Ah, yes, just when we think we've got people figured out, they amaze us.

A Runner duck

Duck Tales

Part One: Protecting the Ducklings

Huey, Dewey, and Louey, our ducklings

I enjoyed sharing the experience of hatching duck eggs with my students and would bring the ducklings home on the weekends or over breaks so my family could also be entertained with their antics. A friend gave me Runner eggs, a breed of duck which stands nearly upright and whose bodies are made in such a way that they can't fly away. I knew this project would be an adventure. And I was right.

This year three ducklings hatched, and the fourth graders named them Huey, Dewey, and Louey. My husband designed a duck pen using four-foot high chicken wire fence. He included a kiddy pool and a predator-proof duck house, which we called the box, to lock them in at night. The box was necessary since it was possible for a cat, raccoon, fox, or coyote to climb the fence, or a bird of prey could swoop in and snatch one of the ducklings.

One afternoon, we heard panicked duck cries. Louey, the youngest, had freakishly gotten his leg trapped between a rock and the ramp. Frank thought the leg had been dislocated, and he tried to put it back in place. Afterward, I set Louey in the box with food and water. He wouldn't eat. Finally, I closed the three inside for the night.

In the morning, I dreaded walking out to the pen. I pictured a scene I'd witnessed before: the weakest one lying on the bottom of the cage and the others pecking it. My neck muscles tense, I walked inside the pen to the box. I held my breath and peered inside. Whew! Louey was standing.

As I filled the ducklings' food dish, Louey walked out of the box, with only a slight limp.

Frank had repositioned the rock that had caused Louey's injury and today, he nailed seven wooden cleats onto the ramp so it was easier for the duck-lings to climb in and out of the box.

Since their pen was small and I wanted them to learn about the world and explore, that afternoon I set them outside of the fence. Louey seemed determined to keep up with the others and joined them as they pecked at my yellow shoes, explored the flower garden, and finally settled in to search for worms and other tidbits in the mulch pile. They were pecking away when I spotted a wild cat.

Crouched low in its hunters' pose, it prepared to attack. I stood frozen in panic for a second, enough time for it to stare me down. My instincts kicked in and I yelled, running until I stood between it and the ducklings. I curled my lips in that universal mother snarl that means Don't you dare. But it slipped past me and streaked for them.

They scooted away just in time, and I chased after the cat, waving my arms wildly and yelling, "No! Get!" The cat took a second look at this screaming lunatic and decided to streak off for the safe woods.

That night I was still shaky when I locked the ducklings inside their box. At 4:30 the following morning, Frank woke me. "Can you hear the crows?" he asked. "I wonder what's going on."

Getting up in the middle of the night with our babies had also been my responsibility, and I threw on a robe and grabbed a flashlight.

Opening the outside door was like watching Alfred Hitchcock's *The Birds*. Swooping winged silhouettes and raucous caws filled the predawn world. Had the door of the box somehow opened leaving the ducklings unprotected?

My heart thudding with adrenaline, I shone the flashlight and hurried to their pen. The box's door was closed. Through the mesh screen I spotted three ducklings huddled together, on high alert, but safe. I searched the brush for a wild cat, raccoon, or coyote. What was stirring at the fringe of woods intent on getting my ducklings?

They were safe for now, but my instincts told me this wasn't over.

Part Two: Spreading Their Wings

*T*raveling with a pet taxi filled with three half-sized ducks made for a stinky van ride to our cabin 200 miles away. The car's pine-scented air freshener wasn't enough to mask the smell, and we switched from breathing through our mouths to opening the windows. The ducks' occasional peeps sounded a bit like nagging children. "How much longer? Are we there yet?"

After arriving, I set the brooder near the lake's shore and opened the door. My "what if" mode kicked in. *What if the ducks dart for the lake, swim away, and I never see them again? What if one of the many coyotes or foxes I'd seen in this area are sniffing about? What if a hawk or eagle spots them, swoops down, and snatches one?*

As scary as those questions were, I certainly wasn't going to keep the ducks in a small pen or cage the rest of their days. It was time for them to spread their wings. I tilted the brooder, encouraging them to come out. They didn't seem interested in escaping or even splashing around. "Am I going to have to put my swimsuit on and teach you how to swim?" I asked.

Dewey quacked in answer. Her quack confirmed my suspicion that she was the only female. It's a little-known fact, but only hens quack. Huey and Louey made softer squeaks, grunts, and gabbles.

I caught Huey, walked out on the pier, and lowered him to the water. He squawked in protest and frantically swam back to his siblings.

Frank joined us as the duck trio contented themselves with picking at the bugs underneath the shoreline plants. Huey found a long earthworm and ran from Louey and Dewey, gobbling as much of it as he could, but Louey snatched the dangling end. I wondered what they'd do when they got to the middle of the worm. Louey pulled, got the whole thing, and sprinted away.

They'd caught their first food and were fighting over it. Frank and I looked at one another. We couldn't have been more proud.

"Well," I said, "they don't seem to want to swim. Maybe tomorrow they'll want to kayak."

The next afternoon, Frank handed me Huey, the first born. While sitting in the small craft, I didn't have the greatest balance. The size and shape of a bowling pin, Huey used his strong webbed feet to push out of my hands. He scrambled around on the kayak's floor causing me to lurch to the side and nearly fall in.

Huey jumped overboard, swimming for shore, squawking all the while. I didn't need to know duck language to figure out he was mad. As soon as he reached land, he organized the troops. He led the protest march into the woods, gaining speed as they neared the dense undergrowth. Since I was still stuck in the kayak, it was up to Frank to jog off after them.

Using his old defensive linebacker skills, Frank got ahead of them, steering them back to where their pet taxi sat near the pier. We debated about locking them up while we kayaked, but decided against it.

When we returned, I didn't see them at the water's edge. "They're gone," I cried, searching the tall grass. Then I heard a soft squeak. Three indignant bodies were finding solace in the pet taxi that had been their brooder. They lifted their heads as I approached and their squawks seemed to say, "Don't ever try anything so stupid again."

"Oh, you guys. I'm sorry. No more kayak rides. I promise."

I filled their food and water containers and they left their pet taxi to eat. Afterward, they waddled over and pecked at my feet. I was forgiven.

Part Three: The Cycle of Life

*A*s adolescent ducks, Huey, Dewey, and Louey had their sweet and their not-so-sweet moments. One evening at 8:00 (their usual bedtime) they were still playing in the water garden, so I let them stay up longer. I lost track of time and a half-hour later, while working in the kitchen, I caught sight of them. They had waddled up to the house, three in a row. They stood just outside the back door and made their impatient call.

"Oh, are you ready for your snack before bed?" I asked.

Qu-ank, qu-ank.

"Okay." Reminding me of a favorite classic, *Mr. Popper's Penguins*, the ducklings followed me in a perfectly straight line to their pen. I gave them a couple scoops of feed and refilled their kiddy pool. After they ate, they walked up the ramp to their box. I wished them a good night, then secured the door.

"They are so sweet," I told Frank.

The following afternoon, they proved me wrong when they tested the limits. I'd allowed them to roam in our backyard. Frank was on duck duty and caught sight of them running down the hill to the neighbor's goldfish pond. He called to me and I rounded them up, scolding them all the while.

Louey, the black one who'd gotten his leg caught, was slower getting into the box.

The following day, I had them outside the pen while I gardened. Ducks eat mosquito larvae, flies, and garden pests such as slugs. They also eat weed seeds. But the main reason I wanted them to have freedom was so they'd learn about their world.

I was to regret my decision. I was in the front yard when I heard their frantic calls. By the time I'd sprinted to the back, a wild cat had grabbed Louey, the weakest, and sped off.

The guilt a person feels at a time like this is overwhelming. Deep sadness washed over me. Louey was gone, and it was my fault.

I penned up Huey and Dewey. They quickly climbed the ramp to the security of their box.

Frank and I had a discussion. Until we could build a safer pen, we decided to set a live trap for potential predators. We'd set one previously and had caught a feral cat, but I'd persuaded Frank to let it go. This time I would not.

Frank and I baited a live trap with two egg yolks. That night I couldn't sleep since I visualized an animal panicking in a trap. I wondered what we'd do if we caught a 'possum, a skunk, or a mother raccoon. How would I feel about taking it away from its babies?

At 4:30 in the morning, I heard yips. A fox! We'd trapped a fox! Heart thumping in time with the yips, I threw on a robe, grabbed the flashlight, and walked toward the trap. I now recognized the yip as our neighbor's dog. The live trap was empty; eggs untouched.

I brewed up some coffee and watched from the window. A mangy tiger-striped cat slunk past in the early morning light. Had this been the one who'd gotten Louey?

I sipped my coffee and thought of tenacious Louey. I remembered how he'd determinedly used the ramp and special steps so he could keep up with Huey and Dewey. I, too, would persist. A plan formed in my mind. Tonight I'd try a bit of tuna in the live trap. I'd do whatever it took to protect my ducks.

Part Four: Hiss, Growl, and Flying Fur

*A*fter losing one of my young ducks to a feral cat, my husband and I set a live trap near the duck pen. We talked with neighbors and we brainstormed solutions. Captured cats could be fixed and then returned to the wild, but they'd still be a threat to songbirds and the young ducks. It was a difficult decision.

At dawn, I wasn't sure if I wanted a cat to be in the trap or not. I creaked open the back door. A different feral cat, this one gray and white, paced inside the trap.

When my husband and I picked up the trap, the cat hissed and growled. An ache in the back of my throat, unsure of the animal's fate, I helped Frank carry the cage to his truck and then drop it off at the city pound. The Humane Society would pick it up from there.

That evening, while Frank and I stood in the backyard talking, Huey and Dewey penguin-walked up to us and made duck noises that told me they were hungry.

I gave them their bedtime snack and tucked them into their box. My heart heavy, I set tuna in a second live trap. Until the ducklings had a large pen with a roof, live trapping seemed like my only way to protect them.

The next morning, Frank I were amazed to discover that something had rolled the trap, tipping over the food and spilling it on the ground. The animal had eaten the food without ever stepping inside the trap. Had it been a wild cat who'd gotten trapped before and learned from the experience?

We were not to be defeated, and that night Frank pounded a stake through the trap so the animal couldn't tip it over.

The following morning, in the dim light, I peered in the trap and saw a huge bundle of fur. The animal filled the entire cage. This was no cat!

At first, I thought it was a badger. Then, as I got closer, I saw it was a raccoon. It lowered its gaze at me in a defeated expression. Resigned to its fate, it looked simply sad.

I was sad, too. Sad and reflective. How is it that the life of my ducklings is more valuable than the raccoon's? Why do I get to choose?

By the time my husband joined me, the coon had changed temperament. It had managed to dig, flinging dirt around, and was in an attack position. We wore protective gloves to carry the trap to the back of the pickup. As Frank rumbled off for a location far from my ducks, I hoped the 'coon wouldn't cause problems for others. I'd never have guessed this duck project would take me on such a roller coaster.

Part Five: Runners Run No Longer

Huey and Dewey, our young Runner ducks, thought they were human. They loved to swim in the cabin's lake (still keeping close to shore, though) and would walk into their pet taxi to be tucked in at bedtime.

One day, my husband commented to our four- and six-year-old granddaughters on how fast the ducks could run. Not wanting to be second best in Papa's eyes, the youngest said, "I can run faster than they can."

The older said, "I can run fastest of all. Let's go!"

Four human feet tore off down the hill. Four webbed feet blurred as Huey and Dewey motored after the girls. Arms thrashed. Wing feathers flew.

The girls won, but the ducks didn't seem to mind. As the girls jumped around and giggled, the ducks flapped their wings and made their excited duck sounds. I realized Huey and Dewey saw the girls as bigger duck siblings.

The ducks were back home and enjoying pecking at plants by the water garden when I noticed Huey didn't have his usual zip. Still, I was unprepared and shocked to open their box the next morning and find him dead. *Why? How? What?* It hadn't been a predator this time.

To make matters worse, Dewey, who usually splashed about in the pond, darting here and there looking for interesting tidbits, simply lay on the ground with no interest in her food. She cocked her head at us, as if wanting help and comfort. Was she mourning her buddy? Should we give her back to the farmer who'd given us the eggs so she could be with other Runners? Was she sick with whatever caused Huey's death?

My husband bought Dewey minnows, a favorite treat, and she chowed them down. Our hopes rose, but that evening, she simply lay in the box, head tucked under her wing, and slept. That night, I had to carry her into the pen. The next morning, she, too, was dead.

Hoping to find out the cause of their deaths, I talked to a vet, to the farmer who had given me the eggs, and finally to someone at the pesticide control center. I told them my husband had fertilized the lawn, but he'd taken care to keep it away from their habitat in the water garden. I'd sprayed for Japanese beetles and insects, which were eating the leaves of my weeping cherry tree, hollyhocks, and hostas. *Hostas!* I'd sprayed the hostas near the water garden.

Using a magnifying glass, I read the fine print on the container. It stated "Birds, especially waterfowl, feeding or drinking on treated areas may be killed." I'd sprayed this product with no thought of the bees, birds, or Huey and Dewey. I vowed from then on to examine labels before buying pesticides.

I will miss the Runners' good morning gabbles, their splashing and diving about, and their humorous escapades.

We eventually built a large, chain-linked pen that Frank and his friend Harold roofed with mesh to keep predators from climbing in. Harold's wife, Mary, knowing how badly I felt about the pesticides, gave me a beautiful statue of a duck. It sits on my porch, facing the water garden and keeping sentry on all who pass our way.

Part Six: All I Really Need To Know I Learned From My Ducks

(with apologies to Robert Fulghum)

*A*ll a person really needs to know isn't necessarily in the academic standards or curriculum. I've learned true wisdom from my pet ducks. Here are just a few of the truths I've gleaned:

- The first one out of the egg has the advantage.

- Every day is an exciting, new adventure.

- If it doesn't taste good or isn't healthy, spit it out!

- Downy feathers become pinfeathers become tail feathers in a flick of a wing beat, so it's best to savor the moments.

- There are many foxes out in the world, but being penned up all the time isn't any way to live.

- It's best if at least one of the flock is on guard.

- When you feed creatures, they will follow you anywhere.

- If you make a mess, someone has to clean it up.

- Even when you're rained on, you can find a silver puddle.

- Preening to impress the flock is worth the effort.

- Birds of a feather do stick together, but when others want to join the flock, invite them in.

- When the bugs are getting to you, you might have to open your beak and snap back.

- Relish every little sunrise and sunset. Tomorrow they may be gone.

- Simple pleasures such as a symphony of morning bird songs, a view of glistening spider webs, and the feel of sunshine on the back are hard to top.

- It's great to stretch your wings, but you're never too old to enjoy being tucked in at night.

- And finally, life is much better with buddies.

Amy and the Runner ducks

Musings
Moth Lives on Tears

Lobocraspis Griseifusa.
This is the tiny moth who lives on tears,
who drinks like a deer at the gleaming pool
at the edge of the sleeper's eyes,
the touch of its mouth as light as a cloud's reflection.
—Ted Kooser

I have seen many wondrous sights in nature. When I was a teenager, hiking with my father, I glanced up at a nearby snow-covered hill and saw a brilliant red fox. I took in every strand of its bright fur, its alert ears, and moist eyes. For a second before it darted away, we looked at one another, and something clicked for me, linking me into the chain of life.

After that moment, I paid closer attention to the mysteries in nature, marveling at all I could see and all that wasn't revealed.

Blazed in my memory is the time a few years ago, while skiing through the Northwoods of Wisconsin, that I caught sight of a bristly porcupine climbing a tree and glossy brown otters playing in the snow.

I've observed turkeys strutting and ruffed grouse drumming, a rare Hawaiian goose honking, and a mongoose prowling, but I've never felt a moth, whose mouth is as light as a cloud's reflection, drink from my tears.

I've kayaked next to a beaver, flinched at the gunshot-like slap of its tail against the water's surface, found its lodge, leaned my ear toward that cozy hut made from sticks and mud, and heard the sound of the young, mewling like newborn kittens.

I've been privileged to watch otters play and hear beavers mewl, but I've never had a moth uncurl its proboscis and take life as it sips away my tears.

I've seen mint-green Luna moths flying in the moonlight and watched hatching Painted Lady butterflies unfurl their wings. I've spotted mated turkey vultures flying into their cave nesting site. I've witnessed young great horned owls peer over their nests as if anxious for their adult life to begin. Mating eagles and Sandhill cranes have performed elaborate courting dances in my presence.

I've walked the same hiking paths as elk and buffalo. I shared a blueberry patch with a black bear. I've slept within feet of roving wolves and moose. Yet I've never had a moth alight on my cheek while I slept and drink at the gleaming pool of my tears.

Or have I?

Silent Rock

I felt it again yesterday—the heartbeat of the woods. Does the pulse I feel from this valley called Silent Rock come from all the creatures watching as I walk down their sun-dappled trails? Does it come from the bubbling spring that feeds the stream? Or does it come from all the past people who have lived here? Did they, too, enjoy watching it change with the seasons?

In the winter, icicles hang frozen as if time stopped the instant they formed. I imagine similar icicles outlining a dome-shaped wigwam where

Ho-Chunk villagers gather. They huddle near the fire telling stories or playing games. On the longest night of the year, they would have hours for such activities.

In the spring, the dogtooth violets come out. I pick them and envision a girl stooping to do the same. She weaves them into a crown, then laughs at something her long-haired friend says. The violet-laden girl places the crown on her friend's head and they dance in the sunshine.

In the summer, I look up toward the ridge. There, in the trunk of that pine tree, I visualize the face of a Ho-Chunk hunter. I imagine him preparing arrowheads while his wife weaves a basket. Two children chase one another around the trees and up and down the slopes, laughing.

In autumn, I listen to the geese migrating overhead and wonder if the hunter's arrow could bring one of them down. The fast-moving stream evokes the picture of a young boy tying a hook made from a goose's wishbone onto a string of sinew. He baits the hook, then throws it out where it's swept downstream. He doesn't have to wait long before there's a tug and he pulls in a shiny trout.

Silent Rock is misnamed. The aura surrounding the place speaks volumes to me.

Best-Laid Plans

A friend was in the midst of cleaning up after a garage sale when I stopped by.

"Whew!" she exclaimed. "So much to sort through and haul off."

"I had my last garage sale a few years ago," I groaned. "They're so much work."

She nodded. "I wouldn't have had this one, but I wanted to get rid of an armchair. A neighbor offered to partner with me, and we began to find all kinds of things. It ballooned. The funny thing is, I sat in the chair during the sale. I remembered how comfy it was and kept putting a higher and higher price tag on it." She laughed. "At one point a woman seemed really interested, and I hid the price tag. I ended up moving it back into the house."

Best-laid plans, I thought on my return walk home. *Good thing I've never had any ideas that got out of hand.*

I arrived at my backyard water garden, lingering over the extensive flower beds. This project had begun simply enough, I realized. I'd seen hollyhocks against the white fence of a downtown bed-and-breakfast and had to have some of my own. I started by trying to figure out where the white fence would go. Two and a half tons of dirt later, I planted a few hollyhock seeds in one of the several new garden beds. Since then, I've spent hundreds of dollars in annuals, perennials, bulbs, patio blocks, an irrigation system, and a glider so I can sit and enjoy all I've created.

I walk over to the arbor where bittersweet vines twirl enticingly about. Next I journey to the new flower boxes where morning glories, sugar snap peas, and sweet potato vines drape down from the freshly painted retaining wall. More vines climb up the new tepee structure that I visualized the grandchildren using as a secret fort.

I move on to a large perennial bed where a swallowtail butterfly drinks from a cone flower, and a rose-breasted finch perches in the sparkleberry tree. I sample a couple of the star cherries from the first fruit tree I've ever tended, but save most of the perfectly ripe, bright-red cherries for the birds. I sit on the glider, a weeping pussy willow cascading down behind me, and watch a bright yellow finch flit about. I plan how I want to prune the weeping cherry so it keeps its delightful shaggy shape, and look forward to the Pampas grass's promised white plumes. This winter, I may watch how the rising sun highlights those feathery plumes and contemplate my best-laid plans.

Hey, I realize. *Where are the hollyhocks against the white fence that started this whole project?* I frantically skirt around once more. I find six delightful pink hollyhocks, but I'd totally forgotten the white fence. *Best-laid plans . . .*

The Herons of my Life

*G*reat blue herons have always fascinated me. As a child, my family's house overlooked a pond and we spent many happy hours at the kitchen table watching the antics of wildlife. We delighted in seeing flocks of Canada geese glide in, kingfishers dart down for a minnow, and painted turtles crawl up on their sunning log to soak up the rays.

On rare occasions, a great blue heron would visit the pond. He'd stand in the shallow water for long minutes, waiting for a fish to swim by. It seemed then I, too, was always waiting—waiting to be old enough to ride my bike on the road or get my ears pierced or become a teenager.

As a gangling, long-legged middle-schooler, I could relate to the heron. One summer, while preparing for a gymnastics competition, my father made me a crude balance beam out of a 4x4. I practiced, keeping in mind the heron that uses its wings for balance and can land on the tiniest of branches. I credit my attempts to emulate the heron for my blue ribbon that year.

Growing up along a pond, I had the chance to study how the heron fished. Its beak rocketed down. If it caught a fish, it paused a moment and some-times flipped it around. The heron had sense enough to swallow it head first so the fins laid flat and wouldn't scratch its throat. Every teenager needs positive role models and reminders to use sound judgement. Why not look to the heron?

As a college student, a friend and I visited a heron rookery in early spring. We brought binocu-lars and sat far enough away so we wouldn't disturb the thirty-some nests. I became fascinated with how the males stretched themselves, fluffed, and circled around to show off. With primal croaks and squawks, males and females crossed necks and exchanged twigs for their nest. I admired how both busily worked together to repair and secure the nest, and hoped I would find a like partnership.

As a young mother, I visited another rookery and learned how the adults eat a fish or frog, partially digest it, return to their young in the nest, and regurgitate it into their waiting mouths. As I repeatedly tried spooning squash or peas into my daughter's mouth, I sometimes wished I had the heron's ability to squirt foot directly. It would have saved on laundry.

Several years ago my husband and I visited a heron rookery along a bay and found a beautiful bluish-green heron egg. We picked it up and both held it. Our own children were at the age when they were leaving the nest. Without saying a word, we brought it home and placed it in a special glass case.

The heron continues to be a kindred spirit. As the sun peeks in my office window, I leave my computer. Time to go to the lake and see what my old friends are up to.

The Artist's Spirit

A friend who wrote and illustrated children's books, Marsha Dunlap, died after a long battle with cancer. The first time I met Marsha was during a blinding snowstorm. A small group of us had rented a bed-and-breakfast and hired an award-winning author, Marion Dane Bauer, to critique our work and share writing techniques. Despite the weather, we were not going to miss this opportunity.

My friend Eileen and I drove together, peering through the whiteout at the unfamiliar roads. We shook our heads. *We're crazy*, we both agreed. Schools had closed early, the radio reported the state patrol had shut down the interstate, and the author's plane was delayed. Our writing was important, but was it worth risking our lives? I squinted to help Eileen differentiate road from ditch. We kept going, bucking through mounting drifts.

We pulled into the driveway of the B&B, white-knuckled and shaken. We found out Marsha had called and was also struggling to plow through the drifts.

Throughout history, many people have felt a powerful drive to pursue their art, whether it's dance, music, painting, or writing. Native Americans sometimes worked from sunup to sundown just to survive, yet managed to grab a moment to create beautiful beadwork or baskets. Frontier women, with work-worn hands, squinted in the candle-light, stealing moments to cut leftover fabric and

Marsha Dunlap

design a kaleidoscope of colors for their quilts. Why?

Is it that we long to set ourselves apart by our individual gifts? Or do we hope to bring joy to others? Maybe it's our desire to pass something of ours onto the next generation. Or is it our longing to find beauty in an imperfect world?

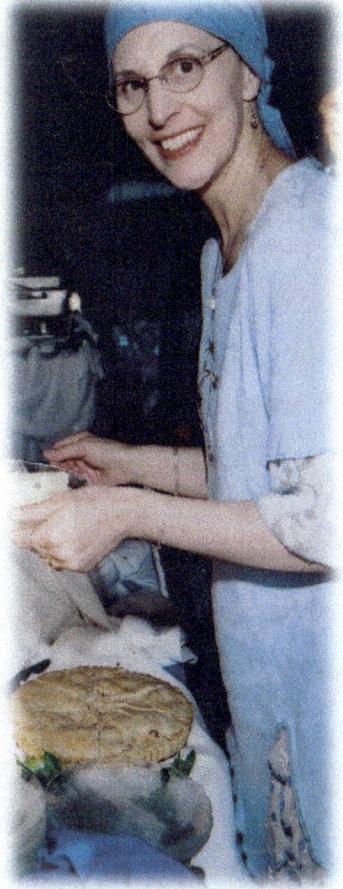

Back at the bed-and-breakfast, the phone rang. Marsha was lost and the owner ventured out to help. After a tense fifteen minutes, we heard the cars pull in. Marsha flung the door open, snow dusting her colorful cap and scarf. "I made it!" Her eyes sparked with warmth and fire. I would notice that same vibrancy in all the years I was privileged to know her.

The last time I saw Marsha, the cancer had progressed. She looked shrunken, but the spark and passion were still there. She told the writing group who met at her home that she'd spent a few minutes painting. I know my mouth dropped. Here she was, having to deal with all the pain and grief of preparing to leave this world, and she had spent time in her studio.

Why do people go to such extraordinary lengths to create? Marsha's work was an essential part of who she was, as necessary as water, breath, and sunshine. Her memory lives on as a testament of a person's drive to create lasting beauty.

Musings

Samples of Marsha Dunlap's art

A Dust Rag Rich with History

Dusting. *Such a boring chore*, I think, as I swipe the lowest shelf of my bookcase. I dust under one of my favorite picture books, *Stars Beneath Your Bed; the Surprising Story of Dust* by April Pulley Sayre. It points out that matter is never destroyed and dust may even contain bits of outer space. I look at my rag. *Might it hold asteroid or comet particles? Mineral flecks from Mars? Dander from an alien creature's lop-eared pet not named Pluto but Earth?*

I continue dusting the natural history section of my bookshelf and realize my dust rag could be collecting a speck of toenail from a tyrannosaurus, a chip from a wooly mammoth's tusk, or a fleck from a passenger pigeon's feather.

As I lift a family Bible, I imagine dusting up a bit of stubble from Moses' beard, a piece of Noah's ark, or a particle from the strap of Jesus's leather sandal.

I dust the biography section next. My rag could hold powder from Ben Franklin's wig, a bit of deer hide from the beaded amulet a Lakota mother gave her son, or exhaust from the bus where Rosa Parks refused to give up her seat.

As I finish with the world history section, I can't help imagining my rag holding microscopic bits of pottery from an Egyptian village, paint chips from a Japanese emperor's temple, or flecks of gold from a California miner's hidden stash.

For fun, I get down on my hands and knees, move the dog bed, and take a swipe on the hardwood floor. Could my rag contain fur from a Madagascar lemur, part of an Alaskan grizzly bear's left front claw, or a bit of my beloved childhood dog's fur?

I eagerly hop up to dust the piano. I could be wiping up the same dust fibers that had once been on Beethoven's piano, Ringo Star's hairbrush, or Elvis's blue suede shoes.

I move the July newspaper, the photo of the American flag catching my eye. My rag may be holding bits of the Twin Towers that exploded on September 11, dirt from a farmer's field whirled away by a dust storm, or fiber from a veteran's uniform.

I pause to reflect. I may be touching a link to one of the thousands of American soldiers who left his or her spouse and children to protect our nation, to the World War II veteran who enlisted after the attack on Pearl Harbor, or to the Vietnam vet. My hand may contain a speck from the American Revolutionist who bravely faced the British redcoats or the Civil War bugler who signaled, "Charge!" Bits and pieces of courage and conviction.

I'm finished dusting. I reverently take my rag outdoors and give it a good shake. Dust particles rich with history fly off, not to disappear, but to resettle as part of the universe once again.

Seasons

Fall, a Beginning of Delights

*M*any people think of fall as an ending, but I've always thought of it as a beginning. For my newly married daughter and son-in-law, it's the dawn of their life together. For students who arrive in classrooms with sharpened pencils and eager attitudes, it's the emergence of new classes, teachers, and friends.

Fall is a perfect time to celebrate. Visitors travel from miles around for our local fall festivals. I look forward to walking around the art fair and chatting with friends I haven't seen over the busy summer.

This autumn, I'll let the cooler weather energize me and enjoy the crisp, sunny days. Hiking under golden leaf canopies or through fragrant red and orange leaves is sure to renew my spirit.

I'll rake the leaves high, delighting in their smell, then laugh while I watch my grandchildren jump in them.

I'll soak in the colors of fall: lavender and cheery yellow mums, deep orange pumpkins surrounding corn shuck decorations, or patchwork lawn scarecrows sitting on golden hay bales.

I'll savor the tastes of autumn, driving to an apple orchard and sinking my teeth into the crispest, tartest apple or indulging in a gooey taffy apple. I'll come home from work to a pot roast which simmered all afternoon or indulge in a favorite fall dessert, pumpkin pie topped with whipped cream.

I'll appreciate the delights of fall fabrics: the smell of leather boots, the feel of corduroys, the look of bulky, cable knit sweaters and tweed skirts worn with those high boots.

Fall is the beginning of fun activities: football and cozy bonfires; bird watching and turkey hunts; and it's the best time for outdoor photography. I'll study how the light plays off the rich colors and take sunlit rides through the countryside. I'll carve out time to bike on roads edged with maples or boat on our cabin's lake where the golden hues of birch and maple reflect in the still water.

Fall isn't an end at all. It's the beginning of a splendid bounty of delights.

Who Needs Turkey?

*W*hat do a naked woman, a baby raccoon, and a tavern ghost have in common? They're all stories to entertain Thanksgiving guests. This Thanksgiving, I'm spending less time cooking food and more time cooking up stories. I figure the food will quickly disappear, but stories will live on.

For appetizers, I'm planning to serve up a tray of giggles. Here's one of my favorites. My husband and I, along with friends Jeanne and Bull, enjoyed a swim in a remote lake. Bull is a big guy and when Jeanne wanted to change out of her suit, she used him as a screen. My husband was putting on his shoes while I absentmindedly dug in the food bag. Finding a granola bar, I offered it to Bull. Too late I realized my mistake. Bull strode toward me. "Ahhhh!" Jeanne cried, scurrying for the bushes.

During happy hour while sipping cranberry wine or punch, I may share the story my stepson, Jon, just told. His three-year-old daughter was with him at Home Depot when she spotted a burly man with long hair, some of which was in braids. "Daddy," Vanessa said in a loud voice, "Look! He's a girl." Jon offered a smile and thankfully the beefy man had a sense of humor.

While spreading cheese on crackers and butter on pumpkin bread, I plan on offering another story hors d'oeuvre. Friends of my aunt and uncle had to shoot a mother raccoon. My aunt and uncle took one of the babies, naming it Squeaky. My aunt fed it milk from a bottle and it even slept in their bed.

That same uncle and my dad shimmied up a tree and snatched three half-grown great horned owls. The boys kept them in the garage and hunted gophers for them. The owls would keep watch out of the garage window and anytime they saw my uncle or dad carrying their gun, they got excited, anticipating food. My dad and uncle raised them to adulthood. When a zoo owner stopped by, the boys allowed him to take their pets.

While passing around the turkey, I may give my guests a question to chew on. "Do you believe in ghosts?" I'm eager to tell the creepy ghost story I recently heard. My friend bought a bar in Wisconsin. After the sale, the previous owner told them the building used to be a church and that a man had hung himself inside. He was convinced the building was haunted.

Sure enough, one day before three witnesses, a trash bin rose chest high. Cold air surrounded the bin and flowed outward. On several occasions, the glass pop bottles shook in their cases. Was a ghost responsible? Whoooooooo knows?

And now for dessert. I think I'll share a sweet story of innocence with a dollop of humor. My friend Penny told me that when she was a second grader, she confessed to her priest that she had committed adultery. She heard a stifled laugh behind the curtain, then a voice said, "Do you want to tell me more about that?"

"I wrote a love letter to this older boy," Penny sobbed. "An adult. Isn't that what the nuns mean by adultery?"

My guests and I will share a chuckle as warm and rich as mincemeat pie.

Ah, yes. Spare me the tight pants and indigestion this Thanksgiving. Instead, let me indulge in a pot full of tales.

Winter's Simple Pleasures

I'm heading to the cabin for the last winter hurrah! The calendar says spring is less than three weeks away. It's time to run a checklist and make sure we haven't missed any favorite activities.

- Enjoy the snow!
- Ski cross country in late winter when the sun's intensity makes it possible to go coatless.
- Snowmobile with a fun-loving group. Or for a quieter time, ride horseback in newly fallen snow.
- Go out on a frosty evening, cup hands and call, "Who cooks for you, who cooks for you-all." Does an owl answer?
- Go on a sleigh ride, swooshing through the drifts.
- Take a hike in the woods after a fresh snowfall and "read" the animals' tracks. Interpret the story they tell.
- Savor the tastes that only winter brings.
- Enjoy steaming tomato soup and grilled cheese sandwiches or a simmering pot roast.

- Steep mulled cider, letting the aroma fill the room. Peel a juicy orange, lingering over the smell.

- Bake molasses cookies and share them while they're hot.

- Come in rosy-cheeked from ice skating and fix hot chocolate with marshmallows.

- Cherish winter's slower pace.

- Curl up with a cozy blanket and enjoy a good book.

- Sit in front of the fire and do the crossword puzzle.

- Enjoy a movie and eat freshly popped corn.

- Soak in a hot tub.

- Be the first to awaken and have the frosty morning all to yourself.

- Spend the morning in comfy 'jammies and the evening in the recliner.

- Hope there'll be a snowstorm so you can hunker down and play cards or a favorite family board game.

- Head outdoors to breathe deeply of winter's fresh air.

- Photograph the beauty of a winter scene such as a frozen waterfall.

- And best of all, listen for the cardinals announcing the coming of spring.

Amy snowshoeing at Bond Falls, Upper Peninsula of Michigan

Spring's Promise

*S*pring hikes, chances to spot deer or hawks, are always favorites, so I was surprised when I set off for the woods with a different plan. Today I would find a patch of woods and simply sit, a suggestion I'd read in a nature magazine. I would try to make it for the recommended fifteen minutes, although I didn't hold much hope.

I found my patch and got comfortable in the old leaves, rustling them around as I settled in. Mmm, the smell. I wondered how to describe it. Musky? Tangy? Earthy? I chose earthy. Now, what word would best describe this time of year?

As I pondered, I displaced some of the forest covering to feel the damp soil. I looked closer. Castings, shaped like tiny footballs, lay at the worms' entrances to their tunnels. Worms work day and night burrowing and bringing up the freshly oxygenated soil necessary for plants to grow. I never took the time to ponder how extraordinary that is!

I stayed quiet and studied the earth again. Those little scratch-like prints--could they possibly be a grasshopper's tracks? An ant scurried past, intent on a secret mission. The wind swept across, stirring both leaves and creatures. I listened. My heart thumped: *lub-dub, lub-dub.* The earth beneath me pulsed: *lub-dub, lub-dub.* We are connected yet I am only one small part of this earth. No more important than the ant or leaf.

A partially sprouted plant lay in a hollow. Inside that tiny seed is all the capabilities of roots that anchor, stems that shoot up, and leaves that can close up at night to retain moisture. Amazing! How must it feel to be a seed underground, to soak in those first drops of rain, to begin to sprout, then reach for the sun?

I scooped up a handful of earth and brought it to my nose. It smelled like . . . like spring, like sunshine, like . . .

I stared at my watch. Could 15 minutes really have passed? I looked around, breathing in every bit of Mother Nature's presence. And that's when I heard it, just ahead in the brush. A rustling sound. A fox? A bear? Approaching me on still-wet legs stumbled a newly born fawn. Its pearly white spots lay in nearly straight lines on its back.

I knew the mother hid nearby, fearful, watching me, and as much as I longed to, I knew I shouldn't approach the fawn. Instead I ran to get my husband and the camera. The fawn was still there when we returned, and then another miracle happened. I squatted down and it stepped toward me, stretching its neck to nuzzle my fingers, then licking my hand.

My eyes teared up. I was simply a small part of this planet, a partner with this newly born fawn. The fawn took one last look at me, then turned and walked away on already steadier legs. I took a deep breath, and that's when I found the perfect word for this time when life begins anew. Promise.

Summer Thrills

"*I*t's time to sky coast," the announcer at the Wisconsin Dells attraction called. "Buy your ticket now!"

The summer night was balmy and, with my husband and good friends Jeanne and Bull along for a night of adventure, I had to say it. "Let's go." Jeanne and my husband (who's never been keen on rides) surprisingly agreed. Bull, however, took one look at the 100-foot tower and passed.

"We've had a three-year-old sky coast and a 92-year-old man take the plunge," the announcer bragged. "We've never had a dissatisfied customer and we never will. Of course," his voice dropped to a conspirator's whisper, "the ones who don't survive can't complain." A man near me chuckled.

I nudged Frank and the three of us joined the line. After a young couple on a platform were strapped in, the bar in front of them tilted forward and they were hanging from complicated looking cords. Their bellies facing the ground, a heavy cable pulled them to the top of the lighted tower. Once there, the announcer called to them, "On the count of three pull the rip cord. One . . . two . . . three!"

The couple plunged down. Screams of terror echoed in my head.

As I handed the attendant my ticket, thoughts turned toward frayed cables, a recent amusement ride accident that had made the news, and my living will, which says not to keep me on life support if there isn't a chance I'll have quality of life. "So," the attendant asked, "who here wants to pull the rip cord?"

Silence. Frank and Jeanne looked at me. I'd gotten us into this. "I will," I finally said, not recognizing my own voice.

"Okay!" the attendant exclaimed. "You need to be on the right then."

The attendant strapped Frank, Jeanne, and me in. Then our bar titled forward, suspending us. The cable slowly pulled us up. I turned my head skyward but couldn't enjoy the beautiful crescent moon and stars illuminating the night sky. We were climbing higher and higher!

"Mistake," my husband muttered. "Big mistake."

Could we ask to be lowered back down?

As if reading my thoughts, the announcer called, "There's only one way down." With a lurch, we stopped at the very top of the tower. The crowd of people below were so small I couldn't make out faces. A huge pile of rocks lay directly below us.

"It's time to sky coast," the announcer cried. "One . . . two . . . three . . . pull the ripcord!"

Why had I agreed to be in charge of the ripcord? What if I got so scared I threw up? What if the cable broke? What if we fell face first on the pile of rocks?

I clenched the cord. There's only one way down.

I pulled.

Whoosh! The sudden drop felt like what I imagined parachuting out of an airplane would be like. My mouth opened, but I couldn't utter a sound. We're going to hit the rocks!

Then, millimeters before impact, or so it seemed to me, the cable caught. Up, up, up. Hanging in midair for half a second, then whoosh, dipping down again. I spread out my free arm. Swish, swish! I transformed into a hawk, swooping down swiftly then rising above the clouds. Up again, higher and higher, above the buildings and trees, then sailing back down again.

Whoa, what a rush! I looked over at Jeanne. She still had her eyes tightly shut, her fists clenched onto Frank and the cable lifeline.

High then low, up then down, back then forth. The moon and stars and city lights all looked friendly now. Jeanne, too, was smiling either from the pleasant swinging sensation or from knowing she'd survived.

The chair slowed and the attendant freed us. We headed to our car. When I raised a questioning eyebrow at my husband, he muttered, "Never again."

As for me, I won't be bungee jumping or riding the scariest roller coaster right away either. But there was that travel brochure featuring an excursion that included climbing an Alaskan glacier. And I'd love to snorkel in a coral reef. Maybe I'd swim alongside stingrays, sea turtles, or dolphins.

Summer thrills? Bring 'em on.

Amy sharing a moment with a dolphin

Favorites

Growing Wings

*I*t was late fall when my six-year-old granddaughter, Maria, hurried up the walk and asked, "Do you have the magic key, Grammy?"

"The what?"

"The magic key to open the door," Maria explained.

Oh, to the upstairs storage closet. I'd forgotten the "magic key" game we'd played the last time they visited.

While Maria and her four-year-old sister Vanessa flung off their coats, I grabbed the magic key, an old charm bracelet, and up we climbed.

"Try to open it, Grammy," Maria said.

I made a show of trying to fit one of the charms into the lock.

"Nope," Vanessa said.

At the third charm, Maria beamed. "I heard it click." She opened the creaky door.

The girls could stand in the dormer storage area, but I had to walk bent over. "A treasure chest!" Maria cried. "We've never looked in here before."

I was about to lift the lid when Maria shouted, "No, Grammy, you have to use the magic key."

Well, of course.

I did, then slowly lifted the antique trunk lid.

Maria paged through the scrapbook Aunt Heidi had made for her beloved pet guinea pig while Vanessa tried on a Halloween mask with goofy glasses and a big nose. After Maria pulled out a magnifying lens, she said, "Let's go fairy hunting."

The girls raced down the stairs, then ran outside to the water garden where they'd spent many happy hours playing with the seven ceramic garden fairies. Weeks earlier, in September, they'd washed the small figurines under the waterfall, named them, and taken them for rides in the green, wooden fairy carriage.

"They're not here!" Maria said, dashing to look in the carriage.

"I found one!" Vanessa cried. "Sitting on the Halloween pumpkin. It flew all the way over here." She laughed.

Maria stared at a flower pot filled with sand. "Grammy," she said in a soft voice, "do you think if we sprinkle sand on our backs that we could . . . that we could grow wings?"

"I'm not sure," I said. "Let's try it."

We each sprinkled sand on our backs.

"Oh!" I said. "I think I feel a tingling."

"Me, too," Vanessa said. "Let's fly to the fairy tower."

We flew to the tower.

Landscape bricks made the base. Three poles laced with string supported the morning glory vines that formed the roof and the perfect secret fairy hideout.

"Here they are!" Maria smiled, picking up Sunflower and Violet. She held them out.

"We've been looking for you," I said.

"They're going to climb the tower." With a fairy in each hand, Maria stepped on a landscape brick.

She stumbled, dropping both fairies onto the cement.

Maria picked up the pieces. Sunflower's head and leg and Violet's wing were broken off. "I didn't mean to drop them, Grammy." Maria's eyes were huge.

"It's all right," I said. "Don't worry. A little glue will make them all better."

The visit was over too soon. Weeks passed. In the hectic Christmas shopping days that followed, the table where I'd laid the fairies was heaped with wrapping paper, ribbon, and battery-powered toys.

On Saturday, I made some progress wrapping gifts and discovered poor Sunflower and Violet patiently waiting for attention. I looked at the toys I'd bought; toys that beeped and buzzed and entertained temporarily, that would be forgotten long before next Christmas. I shoved them aside.

As I gently picked up Sunflower to assess her injuries, I felt a little itch on my back. Then a twinge, then a shiver. I turned my head to look. *Could it be?*

Closet Memories

*W*ith the approach of each new school year, I feel this urgency to accomplish all the tasks I promised myself I'd do during the summer. Topping the list this year was cleaning the back closet.

"I really need to clear some things out of here," I chanted to myself as I thumbed through the hangers. "Ah, here's the denim jacket that I embroidered with a butterfly, daisies, and a sunset." My elder daughter borrowed it years ago when she'd gotten into retro clothing. I discovered it in one of her discard boxes and reclaimed it.

Tucked alongside it is the swirly blue prom dress I sewed with my mother's help. One glimpse of it and I recall my date, who was on the track team and once ran to my house, smelling of sweat and hormones. Ah, first love.

I search through more clothes and find the semi-see-through lace top that I wore with a Laura Ashley flowered skirt to a college event. I'll never wear it again, but I remember feeling beautiful that day. It, too, will stay.

Also on the shelf is my elder daughter's frilly pink party dress she wore on her first birthday. Years later, as a teenager in t-shirt and jeans, she saw it and moaned, "How could you have done that to me?"

I flip through a few more hangers and pause at the mother-of-the-groom dress I wore to my stepson's wedding, and the silk blazer I bought in preparation for my first book signing. Neither will probably be worn again, but for me, having them is like flipping through the pages of time. Clear out this precious collection of memories?

I shake my head and gently close the closet door.

Dogs in Heaven?

*L*osing a much-loved dog can be heart-wrenching. After our teary-eyed daughters found out their beloved dog had died, one of them asked me if Ginger was in heaven.

"I'm not sure," I said, "but our memory of her is still alive. Have I ever told you about the time Dad and I took her duck hunting?"

"No," they said, leaning closer.

"It was a crisp fall day before either of you were born. Dad and I got up at 5 a.m., drove to the country, then hiked a mile or so toward a lovely scene." I recalled mist rising over calm water fringed by trees. "When a flock of ducks set their wings to land, Dad shot. He got one and sent Ginger out on a retrieve. She was within ten feet of the duck when another flock appeared. Dad shot, but so did a hunter with a black powder musket gun. *Boom! Boom!* Ginger turned, swam back scared for her life, and ran off."

"What did you do?" Heidi asked.

"We decided to stay put, hoping she'd find her way back to us. But she didn't. An hour later, we headed for the car. As we wound our way back through the woods, I was afraid I'd never see her again. But she was standing by the car door shaking."

"Poor Ginger," Heidi said.

"And then there was the time I was pregnant with you," I pointed to Heather. "It was winter and Grandpa and Dad took her rabbit hunting. Since her best pal, Pepper, was along, they didn't expect her to take off, but with the first blast, she was gone.

"We searched until dark, tromping through the snow. My big belly made me especially exhausted, and we had a two-and-a-half-hour drive back home for work the next day, so we left. Grandma and Grandpa said they'd keep looking.

"That night, it got down to 10 degrees below zero. Grandma searched in the morning but still couldn't find her. The following night, the next-door neighbor spotted her in a park shelter and tried to get her in the car, but she ran from him. He called Grandma and Grandpa and they spotted her and got her to come. She was scratched and cold, but otherwise unhurt."

"Remember how she liked to go with us when we went cross-country skiing or snowshoeing?" Heather asked.

I nodded, but remembered, instead, how her father had to carry Ginger back from skiing the last time. I remembered, too, how she had moaned in pain from arthritis while trying to climb the stairs.

"Do you have another story for us?" Heidi asked.

"I have a lot of them," I said. "When Ginger was a puppy, she used to snuggle up against me while I read. That is, until she'd see a squirrel out the window. Then she'd run to the door and bark." I laughed. "She loved to chase those pesky red squirrels. Remember how she'd lie in the grass pretending to be asleep so the squirrel would get closer and closer, then she'd pounce?"

The girls smiled and nodded.

"I like to picture Ginger in heaven surrounded by squirrels to chase," I said, hoping my voice wouldn't crack.

"Do you think there are dogs in heaven?" Heather asked.

"I hope so," Heidi said.

I wrapped my arms around my daughters, and we all looked upward toward the sky.

A Milestone Birthday

*T*his month, I'll celebrate a milestone birthday. It's time to start using the good china. It really isn't so bad. *Gulp, gulp.* Just because orthotics and fiber cereals are frequent entries on the shopping list doesn't mean I still can't enjoy life. Why worry that salesclerks now call me Ma'am and ask if I want the senior discount? So what if now, when a hotrod pulls up alongside me and the young man waves to me, it's not to flirt but to let me know that a tail-light's out.

My advanced age represents years of wisdom. I now know that I'll never be a size 8 so why fret over it; that having a colonoscopy is no big deal; that spending an evening in a smoke-filled bar listening to ear-pounding music can't compare to riding a horse on a quiet, wooded trail.

I now also know that I need to ask for what I want; that time is more precious than money; that following your dream isn't just a cliché; and that I don't give a hoot about how Martha Stewart says I should fold a fitted sheet.

I'll probably never see Australia's coral reef or the sun set over Ayer's Rock, but I've watched a cecropia moth hatch out of a cocoon and that's pretty special.

In my advanced age, I now know that little black dress I bought because a magazine said every woman needed one was a mistake for me; that having balance in one's life is important; that making money truly is secondary to feeling I've made a contribution; and that life is heartbreaking, fragile, and precious.

I also know that I still need to work on patience, that I don't appreciate people enough, that it's a mistake to bring a tired two-year-old out for dinner; that I shouldn't let a Dairy Queen ice cream cake defrost overnight in the refrigerator; that I still have more questions than answers; and that I'll never accomplish all I hope to.

It was a gastrointestinal mistake to eat cabbage before going on a long bus ride and an embarrassment not to wear something over my swimsuit when I swooshed down the steep water slide. It's also a mistake not to laugh at my mistakes.

I've attended my kids' college graduations and held six grandbabies. I'm honored to join with talented, inspirational people, and I can still give my husband a rousing competition on the tennis court.

I now know the meaning of words like temporomandibular joint, plantar fasciitis, and fibrocystic, but I also know maxillofacial surgery, customized orthotics, and benign. I know given the chance there's some decisions I'd change, but there are more that I wouldn't.

A milestone birthday such as this needs a totem. I choose the butterfly. By this age, I've been the larvae feasting and growing, I've spun my chrysalis, been transformed, and laid my eggs. I like to hope I've come to the stage in life where I can unfurl the ol' proboscis and sip of life's pleasures, and maybe share some goodness along the way.

Only One Life

$\mathscr{A}$ friend will soon need to leave her home for a senior facility. I can only imagine the range of emotions she must feel as she looks around, deciding which possessions to take and which must be left behind.

At some point, many of us will also need to sort through our worldly goods. I will start in the easiest room, the kitchen. It won't pain me much to clean out the utensil drawer, donating the melon baller and throwing away the messy wad of twist ties. Parting with my coffee maker may give me a twinge, but I'll get over it knowing the nursing home or wherever I'm going won't cut me off.

Winnowing through my gardening tools in the garage will be more difficult. I'll become sentimental and try to avoid thinking about how much I'll miss seeing my stepfather's hollyhocks blossom or my mother's "Jack in the Beanstalk" plant scale the trellis. It would help if I could pass the seeds or perennials on to another family member, and know the plants will continue to thrive.

Cleaning out the basement will be depressing. I'll have to toss out the supplies from my drying flowers phase and donate my colorful paper from my card-making phase. Nostalgia will set in as I bid farewell to my sewing machine and I finger for the last time the yards of fabric representing clothes I never started. I hate to imagine parting with the incubator that hatched out the comical Runner ducks Huey, Dewey, and Louey, and Happy Feet, the duck who liked to kayak alongside us.

I'll have to cull through closets where I'll uncover keepsakes such as a box with cards I've received over the years. Will I have enough courage to toss the birthday sentiments, heartfelt notes from students, and Mother's Day greetings saying I'm "the bestest mommy in the world?"

I'll feel a hitch in my heart as I agonize over what to do with memorabilia like my daughters' worn ballerina slippers.

My mind will wander as I sift through my office, discovering favorite lesson plans such as nature scavenger hunts and using a magnifying lens to study the contents of owl pellets. My mind will flash back when I find old writing files and uncover my previous laptop with its folders of youthful impressions.

And what about all the books I've been privileged to own? Will I take *Christy* by Catherine Marshall, the novel that made me want to become a teacher? How about *The Arm of the Starfish* by Madeline L'Engle that enabled me to experience the exhilaration of swimming with dolphins?

I'll unearth my bulging "idea folder" filled with inspirational notes. How can I throw away undeveloped ideas, such as a teacher donates a kidney saving her student's life or a child falls into a cave entrance and discovers a moonshiner's still? My chin will quiver as I sift through them. I picture my hand bringing the folder to the trash. But wait. Surely I have a bit of room for it. I'm not dead yet. Into the "keeping" box it will go.

Analyzing over 30 photo albums will seem like an impossible task. As I pull out the most precious pictures, I'm sure I'll be overcome with emotions and many stories will flash in my head.

So there I will be—in a sunny room, I hope— surrounded by a few treasured books, my idea folder, and photo albums. When guests stop by, I'll ask, "Do you want to look at pictures with me?"

If they agree, I could begin by showing them a picture of my stepson. I'd tell them about the time Jon gave me a refresher course on how to set up a tip-up for ice fishing. "He said they'd bite better if the minnow's tail was clipped off," I might tell my guests. "He'd left his clipper behind, so he bit the tail off with his teeth. When it came time for me to set up my tip-up, I bit the tail off my minnow, too.

"Jon was shocked, so I explained. 'We get only one life. Only one. I want to live mine to the max.'"

My guests might cringe or laugh or nod. Once they leave, I'll continue looking at the album, revisiting the pages of my life.

About the Author

A retired fourth-grade teacher, Amy Laundrie began writing personal essays because of a desire to share some of her favorite stories and connect with others. Readers have called her stories poignant, humorous, and heartfelt testimonials to a woman's life. They have universal truths and emotions that speak to a wide reading audience. She considers herself a goal setter and is proud of finishing a half-marathon, surviving two wilderness backpack trips and earning a black belt. She enjoys playing tennis, cross country skiing, hiking with her dog Josie, and raising pet ducks.

A Note From the Author

Let's connect. I'd love to hear from you. Stop by www.laundrie.com or my "Amy Laundrie author" Facebook page for updates and a friendly chat.

www.ingramcontent.com/pod-product-compliance
Lightning Source LLC
Chambersburg PA
CBHW070806280326
41934CB00012B/3086